DIGITAL
MELTING

Making Illiquid Real Estate Assets Liquid Through Tokenization

KYLE STEVIE

ISBN Paperback 979-8-218-16368-6
ISBN Ebook 979-8-218-16370-9

Cover Design: Susi Clark of Creative Blueprint Design and Kelsey Weber
Formatting: Creative Blueprint Design

CONTENTS

PREFACE

In 2017, I, like millions of others worldwide, heard about this thing called Bitcoin. It was this magical money that was not created by the Federal Reserve. A group of computer geeks decided that strands of code could be traded back and forth, and they all trusted that it represented an intrinsic economic value of X. It was created by solving math problems. It was the most illogical thing that I had ever heard in my entire life.

That did not, however, stop me from being **very** interested in its meteoric rise in value in relation to the United States' dollar. In a matter of months, one BTC (the Bitcoin abbreviation) went from something like $3,500 USD all the way to $20,000 USD by December. I got in at $15,000. I bought as much as I could, which wasn't all that much. I held on to it as it went to its peak, and then into the "Cyber Winter" of 2018. As the price plummeted, I freaked out and sold once it hit under $14,000 USD. (Over the course of the next 18 months, BTC would drop all the way to around $3,000 USD.)

In the end, I lost money, like millions of others. Oddly, I wasn't upset. Instead of feeling a sense of remorse for being sucked into something so crazy, I felt excited about the possibilities of where the technology could go.

I felt excited because I had dedicated myself to studying not just BTC, but many other cryptocurrencies. I understood that tens of millions of people were participating in a marketplace. A large enough percentage of those people were making significant amounts of money trading tokens. An alternative asset class was blossoming right before our very eyes. This asset class provided instant trade settlements and appeared to cut out the middlemen.

The dark side of cryptocurrency also intrigued me. I learned about the BTC's role in the Silk Road and money laundering. I learned about the power of marketing an idea that the creators had no desire to bring to real life. They merely wrote a pretty White Paper, pumped out some ads, listed a token, and tried to capitalize on suckers buying their tokens only to cash out as soon as possible. They made millions. They also violated numerous Security Exchange Commission Regulations in the process. On top of all that, they could lose over 50% valuation in the matter of a few hours. Craziness.

The thing that excited me the most was the trustless networks they moved in. The technology that permitted trustless trade and automatic settling was what caught my attention as the future. That epiphany came in December of 2017.

Here in Cincinnati, a one-day conference popped up out of nowhere. It was called the "Day for Crypto." It was hosted by a start-up named CPROP. That day, I met one of the founders, Adam Koehler. Adam would become one of my mentors in all things blockchain and has become a good friend.

During the conference, I would be introduced to another guy who would become a trusted source of counsel.

After listening to speakers for the better part of eight hours, I realized there was one guy on stage that seemed to really speak from the point of view that I held. None of this was sustainable without regulatory oversight. The use of blockchain and crypto riding on blockchain networks had the potential to change the financial world, but it wasn't going to be able to happen in some cavalier, "Screw the Man," type approach. Compliance was the key to a long healthy life. That speaker was Michael Hiles.

That day, my life changed forever.

After the conference was over, I sought out Adam at the organized social event and got about three minutes to talk to him. He invited me to the crypto meetups in Cincinnati. I attended every one. They were, like I romantically envisioned, meetings like the great Humanists had in French Salons in the 18th century. There were lots of discussions of theory and potential. There was a lot of guesswork about which company was doing what and which token, or account of value, was on the up, and which was going down.

One night, Hiles, as we refer to him, came down and told us that most of this was all bullshit. Most of those companies were trading unregistered securities and were going to have to pay the piper whether they realized it or not. I appreciated the candor, because I was not completely comfortable with an asset class that was so valuable but based on nothing at the time.

I was also a lawyer and felt far more comfortable playing in a regulated sandbox. Adam had Hiles present his future of crypto a couple of weeks later. His vision, it turned out, was not "crypto" at all. Rather, he was all in on the underlying potential of blockchain to revolutionize financial markets by limiting, or eliminating, friction in all types of financial settlements. Trades of shares would be instantaneously recorded and settled in a matter of seconds. Municipal bonds would be able to move between holders just like shares do now. He presented his pitch deck for his start-up, 10XTS. I was as in as I could be at that moment.

Between those two, I have learned so much more in regard to what can and can't happen with cryptocurrency. Adam is a visionary who sees the highest potential for an idea before anyone else does. He also studies the opportunities and drawbacks. He has connections all over that can tell which token is all hype and which has a working project with great potential.

Hiles is the rare computer genius who understands financial markets and regulations in equal parts. He is part of a crypto fund that has overwhelmingly outperformed, the returns of the S&P. (He's a realist. Just because most of it is bullshit doesn't mean that it all is.)

I invested in CPROP in December of 2018 and 10XTS the following July. While CPROP is still a work in progress, their business plan was badly injured by China's focus on limiting foreign real estate investment policy in 2020.

10XTS on the other hand has the opportunity to corner the tokenized security interest compliance market. My belief in Hiles and 10XTS is why I'm writing this book. It is three parts education, one part marketing. The company leaders have met with Congressional members, SEC Chairpersons, and leaders of foreign countries. They have opened an office in San Juan Puerto Rico to be closer to the burgeoning scene of likeminded blockchain companies looking to blockchain to open alternative investment opportunities by making trading on secondary markets easier for and more accessible to the masses.

10XTS at its core uses blockchain to permit the compliant trading of tokenized real-world assets between multiple decentralized Alternative Trading Systems (ATS) or other secondary markets. They are the glue that permits companies trading tokenized assets secondary markets to trust that a token traded on one ATS is not duplicated and sold on another. With the IRS and SEC satisfied, new financial markets will open, permitting instant settlements while also permitting all members of society to increase their wealth through participation in a world many are currently shut out of. Once completed, Hiles' vision will have come to fruition. Blockchain will revolutionize financial markets as we know them.

I want to add this, and this is the **most** important thing about this book. I would not have written it without the support of Adam and Michael. I also would not have written it without the "support" of my wife, Allison. I put support in quotations because my wife does not suffer fools. I love to procrastinate; it is literally a pastime of mine. I'm the type of guy who looks into the clouds and comes up with killer ideas only to forget about them or just let them die. Her foot was the one that kicked me in the ass for **months** and forced me to "stop talking about it and just write the fucking book."

I couldn't have picked a better drill sergeant and, if I lived a million more lifetimes, couldn't find a better partner, friend, or mother of my children.

I hope that you like the outcome of my experience. Thank you for reading.

INTRODUCTION

The ability of the real estate industry to pivot and adopt technological advances is akin to trying to turn a battleship. It is unwieldy, slow, and requires massive expanses of energy. As a result, it is easy to be at the forefront of a movement but not reach the goal destination for quite a long time. That is where we find ourselves when it comes to the fractionalization of ownership interests in real-world assets, particularly through the tokenization of those interests in real estate holdings. The future is extremely bright at our destination, but it is going to take some massive patience to get there. So, hold tight, and educate yourself on what has the potential to completely change the landscape of real estate investing as tokenization unlocks liquidity and investment opportunities. Now's the time to jump on board to get ahead of the curve.

What is that destination? Imagine if you could take your shares in a private real estate investment trust, or a syndication, and get near instant liquidity by selling some of your interest on decentralized secondary markets. Imagine being able to accumulate more wealth in real estate with each paycheck by buying tokens in properties $100 at a time instead of cutting a check for $50,000.

Well, individual "ships" have already arrived at that destination. Broker-dealers host Alternative Trading Systems (ATS) where they permit people to buy and sell particular security tokens. The issue is that they can only be traded on that individual ATS. Our big ship is traveling to port to make it easier to trade a security token across multiple ATS.

Inertia to change in the real estate industry is almost baked into the character of the industry. A good friend of mine, Adam Koehler, told me about his experience with helping bring Dotloop to life. DotLoop was the brainchild of Alex Allison, a realtor here in Cincinnati. He was sick of the fax machine life. He envisioned a future where contracts would be digital. Digital signatures would be recognized as representations of the real thing, and home sales contracts could be closed with the push of a button. He dreamt of a time when there would be no more signing documents in a windy parking lot on the back of a car and rushing to a brokerage office to fax a time-sensitive document that potentially wouldn't be seen for sixteen hours.

This 115-million-dollar idea seems pretty logical now. However, ten years ago, it was like asking realtors to start selling houses in Ewok (Star Wars reference. You are getting the full nerd effect). Not only was this a new technology, but it was also a new language. As most changes go in an industry, there was massive resistance to the movement. Individual agents had little desire to change how they had successfully operated for decades. It took brokerage houses strong-arming their agents for mass adoption to happen. When it did, the game changed forever, and Zillow gave them an offer they couldn't refuse.

I tell this story to provide background on what to expect with blockchain, smart contracts, decentralized alternative trading systems, and real estate. The world of real estate investing is about to experience a paradigm shift. The heavy work in the engine room is being done; the ship is moving, but it still has ways to go. You are still ahead of the curve timing-wise. Educate yourself now and be ready to disembark into a land of great wealth opportunities through the tokenization of interests in real estate assets.

Finally, as you read this, you must be cognizant of what this isn't. This is not a book about "crypto" even though the word "token" is being thrown around. Rather this is just a digital representation of what already exists, the ownership interest of an individual in a real world asset. It follows the same legal processes as authorizing shares in a company. It is beholden to the same gods.

Compare that to crypto tokens where there are no gods. Even worse, the people who promised to protect your tokens and the cash that you paid for them have shown themselves to either be criminals or really bad at their jobs. The FTX fiasco highlights that.

This book is about establishing fractionalized ownership interests in a real world asset through tokenization and the ability to offer investors liquidity through compliant trading on secondary markets.

PART I

THE WHAT

What in the Bloody Hell Is Blockchain?

This book is an introduction to blockchain and the fractional ownership of a real estate asset through tokenization. As a result, it includes the foundational principles and basic terminology you need to get started. I don't want to bore you. I just want to give the basics so you can go into future meetings with people like Michael Hiles and Troy Vanderburg of 10XTS and understand the premise of their advising as they help you move your real estate offering from, "I'm thinking of tokenizing real estate," to, "Where should we list our token?"

To understand the benefits of tokenization, we need to dive into the fundamentals. Let's begin with *what is blockchain?*

First, blockchain is **not crypto**. We need to divorce that coupling. Crypto relies on blockchain networks, but it is not the only thing that blockchain is used for.

Blockchain is the ledger technology that makes crypto, utility tokenization, security tokenization, and time travel possible. (That last part was the Flux Capacitor, but you get the point.)

Blockchain is a decentralized database that fills many roles that permit peer-to-peer trading and settlement, trustless auto-settling contracts (smart contracts), and immutable (unchangeable) data storage.

Let's break it down. Investopedia defines blockchain as a distributed database that is shared among the nodes of a computer network.[*] As a subpar law student turned inactive attorney **(though not yours, and this is certainly not legal advice nor investing advice)**, I will break this down by element, as we would for legal definitions.

"Blockchain is a distributed database."

As a database, a blockchain stores information electronically in digital format. To the untrained eye, this is nothing fancy. It is just like the computers at work. I save files; they go into the cloud or something, and I can access them whenever I want, right? My IT department can even limit

---

[*] Adam Hayes, "Blockchain Explained," Investopedia, https://www.investopedia.com/terms/b/blockchain.asp.

access to documents and only allow certain people to be in the distribution.

The difference lies in how the data gets into the database and is stored. Most databases are stored in tables within a central server. This allows a company to maintain its data in the most cost-effective manner that it can. The issue is that once a bad actor gets access to the centralized database, you have a Target-sized data breach. Now you get the joy of monitoring your credit history for unusual cards and purchases. The nerds love to give the analogy of grain silos. If you've ever had the pleasure of driving through the "flyover states," you have seen large silos used to house corn. What if a mouse or pest gets into that silo?

To create a blockchain, a group of data is entered and put into a "block." The blocks have a finite capacity and once the block is filled, it is closed with a time-stamped hash. The next block in the chain fills, closes, and is stamped with a time-sequential hash (an encrypted string of numbers and letters meant to be almost impossible to change). This leads to the most significant security asset for blockchain compared to other databases.

"Shared among the nodes
of a computer network."

A node, in this sense, is a computer that has permission to validate transactions in a network and hold a copy of the "ledger" of transactions on the chain. Instead of one silo holding all the grain, there are hundreds, thousands, or (in Bitcoin's case) millions of computers that hold the ledger of the blockchain.

The different nodes require a consensus mechanism to agree that the data being put in is accurate. Consensus is a poly-syllabic word that basically means the majority agrees. Currently, there are two main types of consensus mechanisms for entering and securing data in a blockchain. They are Proof of Work and Proof of Stake.

Proof of Work is what Bitcoin uses. Proof of Work is decentralized. There is no single "main computer" or mainframe center. Nodes on a network can be, and are, located all over the world. (I am going to oversimplify the hell out of this.) A network using Proof of Work uses algorithmic problems that must be solved to close a block of data. Once a node has solved the problem, it sends it to the network. If 51 percent of the other nodes confirm that it is correct, the hash will be created, the block closed, and the node owner will receive some sort of reward (in the case of Bitcoin, a node receives

6.25 BTC for every block it hashes). This helps ensure accurate data and incentivizes node owners to host the network and maintain the ledger.

Proof of Stake is the capitalistic way of creating a hash. In Proof of Stake, the nodes in a network that validate block transactions are randomly assigned based on the number of tokens that node holds. Basically, the more tokens a few nodes hold, the more chances they get to validate a transaction and thus receive the reward.

Regardless of the validation mechanism, every time a block is closed, each node is given an updated ledger of the database. If one node is infiltrated and attempts to change data in a block, it is shut down by the network. This is true if they are trying to hack into block 1A or block 1,000,000A. The nodes revert to the correct ledger, and the blockchain lives on. To continue our nerd analogy, think about a farm with a collection of smaller silos. If mice get into one silo, that sucks, but the entire harvest is not contaminated.

The nature of blockchain allows for information recorded on it to be trusted as the original representation of the data entered in each block because it does not allow for editing, i.e., manipulation. Next is an illustration of how a blockchain network verifies and records data using Bitcoin mining as an example.

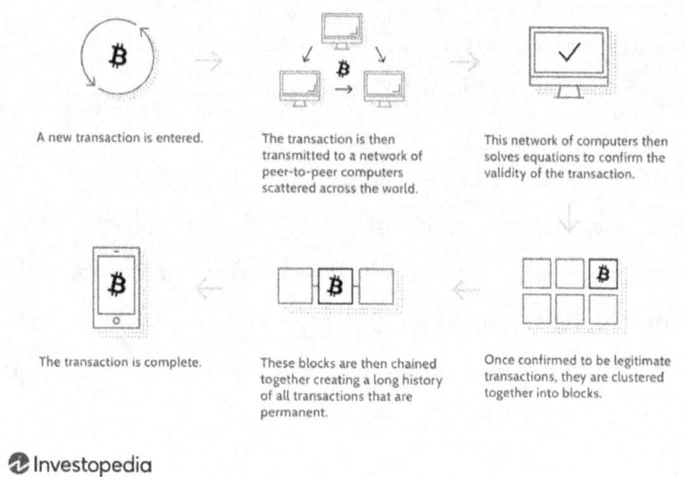

A new transaction is entered.

The transaction is then transmitted to a network of peer-to-peer computers scattered across the world.

This network of computers then solves equations to confirm the validity of the transaction.

The transaction is complete.

These blocks are then chained together creating a long history of all transactions that are permanent.

Once confirmed to be legitimate transactions, they are clustered together into blocks.

Investopedia

Adam Hayes, "Blockchain Explained," Investopedia, https://www.investopedia.com/terms/b/blockchain.asp

Super, Now What?

A blockchain is only as good as the data put into it. As Hiles says, "Shit input is shit output." Additionally, it is only a utility and asset to a company if it provides some tangible benefit. A more secure data storage capability is extremely useful and valuable. It increases trust over the years since your company most likely won't have to send mass mailings explaining that your customers' private information is now in the hands of some 17-year-old hacker in his parents' basement.

In summary, a major point of value for blockchain lies with the increased security for transactions without the need of a third-party verifier (like a bank or PayPal). This, in and of itself, is significant. It is not, however exciting or revolutionary for us — the non-computer nerd population.

What should, and will, excite us is the ability to tokenize a real-world asset and have trust that the token represents the value of the asset. ("Tokenized property interests" is a phrase that is making the rounds to describe this. I don't use it in this book, but I wanted you to know that it is a different title for the same play.) Going a step beyond this, we also have faith and trust that our legal documents and identities that prove real-world ownership are pegged to that token, and every transaction we make is properly recorded and stored. That is thanks to blockchain.

Did I lose you? This book should come with a gram of Sativa gummies or Shrooms in all honesty. Some of this, if it is new to you, will take something to help expand the brain passageways. (I have to put a disclaimer in here. I don't do drugs. I am merely making a joke about the difficulty in grasping the material and any help is welcome. Again, just kidding). It has taken me over four years to get enough of a grasp to write this book at an easily digestible level. Taking complex concepts and turning them into simple language is a taxing assignment. I will break it down next.

What is a Smart Contract?

One of the major innovations in contract law that blockchain makes possible is the smart contract. A smart contract is an agreement where terms are written into lines of code. The agreement, or agreements, are entered into the blockchain and distributed across the network. The coded agreement is self-executing in that as terms are met, neither party must perform an action to confer the benefits. They automatically happen, be it the release of escrow or whatever. As an obligation is completed, the nodes in the network are updated automatically.

Time to get slightly legal here. A smart contract must be the coded expression of an offer, acceptance, and consideration. The issue becomes how states will interpret them. Many contracts that fall under the Uniform Commercial Code and state statute of frauds must be in writing. For the sake of coded contracts, the question is, "Does the entering of code constitute a writing"? Does the smart contract violate the requirements of the UCC or statute of frauds and void the contract? That is what many state legislatures have wrestled with or are currently wrestling with.

There is a precedent that states that haven't legislated the legality of smart contracts will accept them as soon as they get around to them. The Uniform Electronic Transactions Act (UETA) of 1999, which forty-seven states enacted, and the Electronic Signatures Recording Act (E-Sign Act) have set guidelines for the validity of electronic signatures and electronic records in interstate commerce. "An Introduction to Smart contracts and Their Potential and Inherent Limitations," is an excellent article to dive into if you want to really understand where state legislators are headed.[*]

As of this writing, at least twenty states have passed legislation or created committees to either define or investigate the use of smart contracts and under what circumstances they will be deemed valid. Needless to say, know your jurisdiction. Again, I'm not your attorney; this is not legal advice. I'm merely stating that until there is a uniform

---

[*] Alex Lipton and Stuart Levi, "An Introduction to Smart Contracts and Their Potential and Inherent Limitations," The Harvard Law School Forum on Corporate Governance, May 26, 2018, https://corpgov.law. harvard.edu/2018/05/26/an-introduction-to-smart-contracts-and-their-potential-and-inherent-limitations/.

language that states adopt, the definition and validity of smart contracts will be open to local interpretation.

Now that I cast a large legal cloud over smart contracts, let's talk about their benefits. The main advantage of smart contracts is that they are trustless. Transactions completed under the terms of the contracts are traceable and transparent. As we mentioned before, they self-execute. For example, you do not need to wait forty-eight hours for an escrow agent to release funds. They can also be written to govern numerous steps in a real estate investment, from purchase to construction to the automatic disbursement of investor dividends. They permit an efficient flow of funds and documents to the stakeholders in an asset.

The beauty of efficiency leads to a second benefit. Efficiency means cost and fee savings. The role of middlemen can be limited if not eliminated. That means your offering and operation can be done at a fraction of the standard cost you currently pay for administrative fees. There is, however, the issue of the upfront cost of creating the smart contracts.

What is Asset Tokenization?

Asset tokenization can be done with all securities. A security is an ownership interest that someone like me possesses in your asset without ever doing anything to help you increase the value or create income from your asset. Basically, I'm making money off your efforts while contributing none of my own beyond my cold hard cash. Oh, and I expect that you will make money for me.

That is easy to grasp for ownership interests in a business. Everyone knows, or should know, what a stock is. For whatever reason, however, there is confusion when people discuss tokening ownership interests in real estate. They envision owning a part of the actual building. That's not it. It is not a digital record of the title. No county clerk recognizes that.

Stated plainly, it is the tokenizing of an entity's ownership interest, or special purpose vehicle (SPV), created to purchase, control, and maintain ownership of the asset

The buzzword term for this is "fractionalized ownership" which I mentioned earlier.

Fractionalized ownership sounds like what is currently in place. I pay $50,000 and have x amount of equity in the project, right? Kind of...tokenization permits you to divide your investors' shares into fractional values. So that $50,000 in interest can be tokenized into 5,000 units at ten dollars per unit. This permits the investor to list up to 4,999 tokens without being cashed out from the investment. This eases liquidity concerns of your investor in the event of an emergency while keeping your SPV in place.

Fractional ownership is possible because of asset tokenization. Asset tokenization is the process of recording a digital representation of an ownership right in a real-world asset on a blockchain. (That is my definition, and it took forever to make it that concise. Writing is hard, but it is a great definition.) Recording my ownership interest of a two-family apartment building on a blockchain allows me to have an immutable representation of ownership that a third party can trust without ever meeting me and my shyster ways. The confidence in tracing the chain of custody of ownership of an asset from purchase to sale creates the setting for a "trustless" verification process that will only strengthen commerce.

What Is an Issuer?

An issuer is "a legal entity that develops, registers, and sells securities to finance its operations."* Finally, we get to talk about you as fundamental in this grand scheme. You are the issuer. There really isn't more to say to this that you don't know. You are issuing a security interest to investors who will do their due diligence to ensure that you are trustworthy. Common sense, really. The hardest role you will have as an issuer of a digitized security is walking your investors through what this all means and how they can get their money back, hence this book.

While I stated that you are the issuer, you will not be working alone. Another company will have to help you create the token. Right now, the industry primarily operates on Ethereum. The blockchain permits the building of apps on that and the easy creation of ERC-20 tokens that can be

---

* Adam Hayes, "Issuer Definition," Investopedia,
  https://www.investopedia.com/terms/i/issuer.asp.

exchanged on the network with other ERC-20 tokens. The issues with ERC-20 are that they are created on the public Ethereum chain, and transaction costs are pretty high. Luckily, Ethereum is not the only blockchain making it easy to create tokens. There is a lot of momentum by alternative blockchains such as Avalanche, Solana, and Poly to provide similar Layer One network functionality at a fraction of the cost per transaction. There are more secure ways to tokenize your offering so that your data stays private.

Whomever you use, and however you do it, remember that tokenizing the offering in a decentralized manner permits you to be the owner of your data. It is imperative that you have that in mind when you speak with providers.

What is an Alternative Trading System?

What is the point of tokenizing an asset? Without the ability to move an interest in the asset, tokenization is just a waste of money. To move the asset, there must be an SEC-compliant market facilitator where people can offer, accept, and receive consideration for the sale of their token (which, remember, is the digital representation of their ownership interest).

A main reason to tokenize an offering is to provide early liquidity for investors without blowing up the legal entity that owns the property, fund, or REIT. Publicly traded REITs already offer this option. Shares in those REITs can be bought and sold on traditional markets. The issue is the legal and auditing overhead that comes with creating and operating a publicly-traded REIT. I will let anyone unfamiliar with them dive in and research. I only bring this up to set the stage for the alternative that I am about to discuss.

The alternative is trading on SEC filing exempt offerings on secondary markets, primarily ATS. ATS provides numerous benefits to over-the-counter markets. One example is the prohibiting of naked shorts of a ticker. They're also less costly as they have much lower listing fees and auditing requirements (not requiring a full Public Company Accounting Oversight Board audit like NYSE or NASDAQ).

Their ability to match buyers and sellers provide liquidity that a market requires to exist, let alone thrive. This helps solve the main issue for selling a tokenized interest in a real estate investment for the near future — liquidity.

A real-world example of an ATS dealing in tokenized real estate interests is tZero. In 2018, Elevated Returns, a hospitality-focused asset management company, decided to raise capital using fractionalized indirect ownership of 19 percent of the St. Regis Aspen resort. The 19 percent was valued at $18 million at the time of the first offer. Elevated then partnered with tZero, an online platform, to create an alternative trading service to give a secondary market to sell the tokenized security. The token, Aspen Coin (ASPD) can be bought and sold on tZero currently. (You can go there and get an idea of what your offering will look like.)

The ability to offer your token on an ATS saves you potentially millions in listing costs. The downside, of course, is liquidity and public interest. A major reason for this is that not many people are familiar with tokenization and where it is taking the real estate investment industry. While the tZero and St. Regis deal happened over three years ago at the time of typing this, the trend has been very slow to be accepted. I believe this is about to change. I'm going to explain why below.

What is a Broker-Dealer?

A broker is an individual or financial services company that enables the trading of securities for other individuals. A dealer is an individual or financial services company that enables the trading of securities for themselves.[*]

If you are one for legal definitions, Section 3(a)(4) of the Securities Exchange Act of 1934 defines "Broker."

Why does that matter to you? In your traditional exempted offerings, **many** General Partners (GP) are walking the fine line of being compensated on a transactional basis. I leave that up to you and your attorney to discuss. What I am saying here is that for a tokenized offering, you will need a Financial Industry Regulatory Authority (FINRA)

---

[*] Lisa Smith, "What Is a Broker-Dealer and Why Should You Care?," Investopedia, https://www.investopedia.com/articles/investing/072913/what-brokerdealer-and-why-should-you-care.asp#toc-putting-it-all-together.

licensed broker-dealer to sell SEC-compliant tokens. FIN-RA protects investors who are putting trust in broker-dealers in which they actually possess the ownership right to the shares the investor is purchasing or selling.

Broker-dealers who act as intermediaries can only place orders. They do not do the settlement. They are paid a finder's fee by the executionary broker who settles the order.

Why do you need a broker-dealer? Well, only broker-dealers can create ATS. That's a pretty important role. It is so important that a broker-dealer must be certified through passing the General Securities Principal Qualification Exam or the Series 24.

For a real-world example of a broker-dealer's involvement with tokenization of real estate interests, we'll do a Jen Psaki "circle-back" to the St. Regis deal. In that deal, tZero is the broker-dealer, and the token is listed on their ATS, which looks a lot like a standard screen you'd see on any brokerage site when checking out a stock's price movement.

Not for nothing, a promising change to the role of the broker-dealer in the digital asset space was proposed by the Security Exchange Commission (SEC) just recently. The SEC created a new role for broker-dealer, or a new type altogether called a "Special Purpose" Broker. Sounds like a Marvel superhero. The Special Purpose broker can **only** take custody, match orders, and/or settle the trade of digital assets. It's a wild new world, one that potentially removes financial institutions like banks from the digital asset custody game. For the legal beagles out there, you can find the commentary here: 86 FR 11627-11632.

What is a Transfer Agent?

A transfer agent is a trust company, bank, or similar institution assigned by a corporation for the purposes of maintaining an investor's financial records and tracking each investor's account balance. The transfer agent records transactions, cancels and issues certificates, processes investor mailings, and handles a host of other investor problems, including reissuing lost or stolen certificates.[*]

This sounds a lot like a good property management group. They handle rent collection, property upkeep, renter complaints, and the like.

The role of the transfer agent (TA) is to record all the information that the SEC and IRS require you show to ensure

---

[*] James Chen, "What Is a Transfer Agent?" Investopedia, https://www.investopedia.com/terms/t/transferagent.asp.

your offering and the eventual trading of your tokens stays compliant.

The transfer agent will receive all notice of settlement for token trades from the executing broker and/or custodian and record them. This ensures that your investors' accounts are automatically updated and accurate. Additionally, they will create all the tax documents that your investors need to file their taxes each year. In the event that your investors lose their keys or access to their tokens (this *will* happen), the TA will be able to reissue the investors their tokens and not shut them out of the value of trading, unlike cryptocurrency where your ownership can be challenged or lost if you lose the token in a hack or breach, or if you lose your keys...

What is a Custodian?

A custodian or custodian bank is a financial institution that holds customers' securities for safekeeping to prevent them from being stolen or lost. The custodian may hold stocks or other assets in electronic or physical form on behalf of their customers.[*]

This is a legally required layer of extra protection beyond the transparency already provided by the technology that your offering is using. Custodian banks maintain your security interest so that they are not lost in the myriad of transactions that occur while a security interest is traded between numerous owners. Presently, the secondary market regulations in the U.S. require some form of custody for a tokenized security to trade in the secondary markets. Self-custody is not accepted by the regulators or licensed intermediaries.

---

[*] Adam Barone, "Custodian Definition," Investopedia, https://www.investopedia.com/terms/c/custodian.asp.

The What

- Blockchain is a decentralized database that fills many roles that permit peer-to-peer trading and settlement, trustless auto-settling contracts (smart contracts), and immutable (unchangeable) data storage.

- A smart contract is an agreement where terms are written into lines of code. The agreement, or agreements, are entered into the blockchain and distributed across the network. The coded agreement is self-executing in that as terms are met, neither party must perform an action to confer the benefits.

- Tokenization refers to the tokenizing of an entity's ownership interest, or special purpose vehicle (SPV), created to purchase, control, and maintain ownership of the asset.

- The legal parties of traditional offerings are the same as the legal parties of a tokenized offering.

PART II

THE WHY

Pros

When I first told people that I wanted to invest in real estate, a lot of them had the same question, "Why in the hell would you wanna do that?" Great question. Why? There must be an incentive to dealing with vacancies, repairs, and awful tenants. That incentive, for 98 percent of people (and that is conservative) is financial. Nobody wants an ulcer for free. The whole purpose of this book is to give you an added tool to unveil a little more of that financial incentive.

There's a famous old saying, "If it ain't broke, don't fix it!" I imagine that many of you are looking at your portfolios of thousands of doors and millions of dollars and thinking, "Now why in the absolute hell would I ever offer this? I have created a mini empire through strategic partnerships. I have built an investor base with a waiting list three deals long. Screw you, Kyle Stevie, and your voodoo blockchains siren call."

Don't worry, I don't take it personally. I envy the position that almost all of you are in. I want to reemphasize that this is not a way to replace your tried-and-true method of capitalistic conquest. I get that many accredited investors are not going to be comfortable with the idea of offering equity on digital exchanges, whether centralized or decentralized. Most operators will want to get the most equity out of the deal as can be had. Usually, that requires keeping a smaller investment pool. If what you are doing is raking in the millions, have at it.

This is, however, a brand new tool that will provide quite a few advantages. How I love the advantages, let me count the ways...I love thou near-instantaneous liquidity; I love thou reduction of investor risk; I love thou reduction in investor minimums...I love thou in countless ways. Somewhere in the Shakespearean prose were some of the advantages to tokenizing security interests in your SPV to create fractionalized ownership.

Reduction in Risk

We briefly discussed the benefits of tokenizing your asset in the lowering of risk to investors, GPs, and any other stakeholder. We did not, however, really discuss the benefits in detail. Let's do that.

REDUCTION IN LEGAL RISK

The first type of risk tokenization can decrease is legal risk to you and your investors. In the "How" section, I will go in-depth regarding how the process works from properly setting up a tokenized offering to legally wrapping up the project. Here, I just want to discuss the benefits

As I mentioned, one of the buzzwords for tokenization of securities is "fractionalized ownership." We defined what it meant. Here I want to rehash why it is important.

In real life, where your money and real estate assets reside, shit happens. People go through things. They may suffer financial, physical, mental, or other setbacks that require large influxes of money to help settle. I know that you know this; everyone knows this. The point that I am making is that chances are something will happen to one of your investors, and they may come to you to get their money back to cover this emergency.

It happens frequently, right? You set up the deal and operate as the GP. You clearly explain the benefits and risks of investing in your project. You pay $10k or more to draft an air-tight Private Placement Memorandum that clearly states there is a risk the investor will lose their $50k buy-in. Additionally, you tell them that returning funds, once invested, will be damn near impossible. At a minimum, it is going to cost thousands of dollars in legal hours to get done. There is the potential that the entity you created will need to be overhauled. It's a pain in the ass.

Here is where fractionalized ownership comes into play. Let's say, worst case, if your investor has an emergency, they currently must divest completely. You are limited, **again**, to only those who are accredited investors and have $50k in disposable income to buy your investor's interest. *Or*, you may have to come up with $50k in the name of investor relations. Either way, it is extremely cumbersome from an economic perspective.

With fractionalized ownership, your investor can list across multiple ATS and decentralized exchanges (not yet, but we are fixing that) and list exactly how much they wish to let go. Your entity stays intact, **no legal fees**! (For clarification, you already paid your legal fees setting up the tokenized offering. Compare that to having to make changes to your SPV). Your investor can now take care of his financial issues and avoid potential bankruptcy. Potentially, they also get to stay in the investment because they only have to sell part of their interest. You are a hero!

REDUCTION IN STAKEHOLDER RISK

A good, kind-hearted developer, syndicator, partner... whatever, will have investor risk at the heart of every decision. They should coin a term like, I don't know, "Fiduciary Responsibility" or something for it (obviously, this is a joke and Fiduciary Responsibility is a **very** real legal responsibility). It is not easy for people to park upwards of $1 million in an illiquid asset and get 7–10 percent back plus a percentage of upside. They are taking a gamble on **you** and **me** as much as they are on the building. So, how does tokenization reduce this risk?

The most obvious way is that, depending on the offering, the investor has a secondary market to dump your crap deal onto as soon as it looks like it is going to turn south. Or, since I'm eternally optimistic, your investor now has an easier way to increase their equity and make more off your deal because they can now buy tokens from other investors who may have had to sell earlier than they wanted. They reduce their risk of losing big, and they can reduce their risk of missing big by being able to use the secondary markets. It may also quicken your capital raise. Investors may invest more during the raise if they know that they don't have to park their money for five to seven years.

What's more is that the reason the investor will feel more comfortable buying more tokens is the second way that we reduce investor risk: transparency. There is very little guesswork with property valuation in real estate. It is as simple as finding the Net Operating Income and dividing by the market cap rate. If you checked out the Aspen Coin (ASPD) on tZero, you would have noticed that underneath the graph is a list of monthly financials and updates. If I were you, I'd go a bit deeper and provide the current cap rate of the market provided by a company such as CoStar or another large commercial brokerage. This data allows your investor to make real-time decisions because they have real-time value for their position. Try making such sense of Dogecoin or 99 percent of the stocks on Robinhood.

Coupled with transparency is the immutability of blockchain, as we discussed above. Once a block of data is closed, and a hash is created, it's game over for any edits without a consensus of stakeholders agreeing to the changes. Records cannot be tampered with, and they cannot be lost. Need to change numbers quickly to show a loss for the IRS and risk becoming a bad actor or hurting the entity? Sorry Dirtbag GP, not going to happen because it can't happen. As an investor, there is no other type of investment data retention that offers the safety of real-time valuation and immutability of records.

Since we are on the "reduction in risk" train, let's go down the line a little more. Let's say that due diligence took longer than expected or a big investor bailed, and you have two weeks to close. What if you can't find a replacement in capital? The risk to your other investors is that they potentially miss out on a cash generating asset. What is one potential way to stop this from happening?

Depending on your offering, you may be able to advertise to, and accept, non-accredited investors. More investors allow you to lower the investment minimum. Investors will no longer need to bring $25,000 to $50,000 to participate. While this is not new and used in thousands of real estate asset purchases currently on the internet, the knowledge that your deal will allow investors to enter and exit freely will give you a major leg up on current crowd funding sites. Living in Greater Cincinnati, the heartland of conservative capital, I can tell you that this advantage alone will help developers and syndicators compete. It's not nothing; it's something very significant.

Real estate tokens are advantageous to more than just traditional investors.

There is a subtle advantage for tokenized offerings in that there is a new group of very wealthy people comfortable trading digital currency. This is a new class and breed of wealthy investors. They have made the bulk of their wealth accumulating digital currencies and are riding the wave until it crests, rises and crests, rinse and repeat. They are in their early twenties to early thirties and will never have to work a day in their lives. They know and trust crypto. They have lived with the ups and downs, bubble bursts, and moon calls.

Eventually, they will need to get some sort of tax advantage. That is where you come in. As a holder of indirect ownership in a real estate project through holding tokens in your property, they will be given a K-1. They will be able to receive the benefits of cost segregation and depreciation while also reaping the benefits of rising rents and property values.

What's more, you will provide an interest in the one digital asset class that is tangible. Most crypto currently is based on an Internet of Things, FinTech, or Software as a Service project. Now, crypto millionaires will be able to hold a tokenized security backed by a real-world asset. This provides them with protection if the powers that be decide to pull the plug on crypto. Though many have said there is no way for governments to shut the whole thing down, all it takes is a crackdown of the exchanges to make it extremely difficult for common computer illiterates like myself to get our money back out. That will not be a concern for your offering. If they can't get instant liquidity, they are back to investing in a traditional real estate offering and owning part of a real-world property. They are far better off than if they had kept all their money in some Altcoin waiting for it to hit a rocket ship to the moon so they can "Lambo." (That was all crypto enthusiast jargon if you didn't know, now you know.)

It is not just the newly minted multi-millionaires that have an advantage. Lowering the amount of equity that you must give up to seal a deal is another major game-changer. As a GP, I have quickly learned to stop living in a fantasy world. I once fell madly in love with the Siren's song: "Everyone will love this project. They'll be happy to give you their money at 7 percent with no up-side besides tax advantages." I skipped merrily along due diligence with visions of 100 percent of the profit dripping into my pocket at resale dancing through my head. In only sixty months, my group would have so much money...and then I looked at the calendar.

I was twenty-five days away from the end of the due diligence period and had nothing to show for it. Little by **a lot**, we caved and were able to secure our...wait for it...$255,000 raise with two days to go. I know, I know. Impressive (feel the sarcasm). The point is that we had to give a premium to get people to partner with us and lock their money up for five years.

This dovetails nicely into...

Liquidity Premiums

Investors in publicly-traded REITs pay a liquidity premium due to their ability to trade their shares with ease. The property owned by the REIT is still illiquid, but the investor can exit a deal quickly. REITs, however, come with legal costs that most operators cannot or do not want to absorb. As a result, their investors' interest remains illiquid and therefore, they receive an illiquidity premium for taking the risk of tying up their money and the opportunity costs associated with that.

If you do not operate a publicly-traded REIT, you are giving up potential income by offering an illiquidity premium. Where a publicly-traded REIT offers a 6 percent annualized return, you must offer a 7 percent plus upside, or a 10 percent capped return for example.

Tokenizing your offering allows you to eliminate much, if not all, of the illiquidity premium because, depending on your offering, in six months or a year, the tokens become liquid. Investors can leave as they please without paying a fee, penalty, or blowing up the legal entity. With that reduction in risk comes a reduction in the premium you must give up to entice them to invest.

Cutting Out Administrative Costs

As a GP, you aren't playing master of the stock market for your day job. You have to ensure that the property is up and running. You must make good on promises to pay dividends or any type of return. You must add value to the property and your investors' financial lives. (I feel like a 1960s door-to-door salesman selling a new vacuum cleaner), "What if I told you that I could reduce the amount of work by double? Would you be interested then?" Welp, I can't. However, some blockchains can through the use of smart contracts.

As we discussed, smart contracts are basically computer codes that create a self-executing contract between two parties. The terms are written into the lines of code and then governed by a series of "if this, then this" commands.

"Well, Kyle, what can I use this new fandangled technology for?" Distributions to investors to start. Depending on the offering, smart contracts can fire off your distributions without so much as a second guess, "If March 31st comes, send distributions to the following addresses." The beautiful part is that you can also program for K-1 releases and an assortment of other documents/services required either, by, from, or for investors, property managers, and GPs. This doesn't even cover instant settlement of transactions without waiting on the bureaucracy of a bank or financial institute to provide clearance.

Automatic paperwork creation and release is an enormous time-saver. The ability to be flexible in the amount of equity tokenized is an enormous wealth saver. I have briefly mentioned that there will be some blowback from investors who are in the "It ain't broke, don't fix it, Dummy," crowd. That is fine. You can do both. The people from my city are known as Cake Eaters, so this feels fitting: "You can have your cake and eat it too."

As we discussed previously, the interest you offer is a fractionalized interest. You can fractionalize the value of the building into dollars, square feet, square inches, per bathroom...whatever. You can also fractionalize the amount of the project that you want to offer in security tokens. Remember the example of St. Regis? Their offering was valued at $18 million. Do you think a hotel in a little place called Aspen (where the beer flows like wine, where beautiful women instinctively flock like the salmon of Capistrano) only goes for $18 million? Not a chance. They fractionalized ownership of only a part of the building to raise capital. They originally filed to create a single property REIT to list on an exchange. I must believe that fractionalizing the ownership and offering their token saved considerable money through fewer lawyers and less money to list on an exchange.

Altruistic Incentives

Now, finally, we get to a part of the book that *really, really* interests me. The major benefit of fractionalized interests and the listing of tokenized securities is that it creates **economic inclusion**. It opens the door for parties that have been left outside the world of angel investing rounds and apartment syndications. It allows people to create their own miniature real estate portfolios without the fees associated with mutual fund managers. It is like the discovery of fire. It can change lives forever.

Even better than that, it can generate investment in low-cost housing. We have an affordable housing crisis in many cities. Municipalities have either set stupid rent control policies in place or made it damn near impossible to build profitably. I do not know of any builder who is willing to take a haircut to build an apartment complex or forty single-family homes when they could make six figures elsewhere. So, how do we tackle this problem? Stay tuned, I discuss it below.

ECONOMIC INCLUSION

The most hilarious thing about the accredited investor requirements is their arbitrariness. There is no test, no educational qualification. You either are or you are not. I really would love to hear how someone who is earning $150,000 a year through their own labor is less intelligent than someone receiving $250,000 a year through distributions of a Trust that their parents created. Why is it okay for the trust fund baby to reap the rewards of getting into business deals at early stages, but the hard-working person must wait until the deals are offered to the public? The government has no problem allowing anyone to play the lottery or hit casinos. They appear to have had a major wild hair up their ass regarding everyone having access to the same legit wealth-building opportunities as the wealthy.

Luckily, this is starting to evolve. Reg A+ and Reg CF offerings are opening investment opportunities to the general public. Not only are non-accredited investors able to invest in real estate deals at the ground level, but they can invest in businesses as well. The issue was, until March 15, 2021, the capital that could be raised was limited. Those limits have since expanded, so it will be interesting to watch the impact.

Once you have placed your listing, another potential investor group opens up. Foreign investors may be able to purchase security tokens from an exchange that you list on. If you are able to list your token on an exchange like Coinbase, you have now opened the door for people who may otherwise not be able to invest in U.S. real estate. This provides the opportunity to stabilize their wealth that may not be available in their home countries. Vice versa, it could potentially open the doors for U.S. investors to diversify with foreign real estate holdings. I do not know much about my 401(k) other than it holds funds for U.S. and international businesses. Maybe real estate works the same way? I don't know. There are smarter people in the world to answer those questions than myself. (They just aren't as good-looking.)

Granting the opportunity for non-accredited investors to participate and grow their wealth through ownership of real estate is awesome. A wealthier population base is a stronger population base. However, that is nothing compared to the future possibilities of using fractionalized ownership to help ease what is becoming a major crisis of our time.

INCENTIVIZE CONSTRUCTION OF AFFORDABLE HOUSING

We are all aware that the cost of construction is currently going nowhere but up. As a direct result of the rise in costs, real estate projects require that units be rented or sold at prices that are unaffordable for far too many Americans.

It is not our fault as investors. We rely on income from real estate to guide us to our future financial goals and destinations. It is, however, disingenuous to pretend there is nothing that we can do to solve the housing crisis.

The issue is: how do we do our duty for humanity while not killing our own futures? That's where (I *really* hate saying this because I do not find the government, local and federal, efficient at anything) private construction can team up with local housing authorities to create incentives that benefit builders and residents.

The great Sandy Selman of the company CPROP wrote a very interesting white paper titled "The Potential Role of Tokenization in Affordable Housing" that discussed using technology to actually fix a real-world issue. I recommend giving his white paper a read.

I will paraphrase the theme of the paper by saying that we have all been extremely fortunate to be in the positions we currently find ourselves. I was fortunate enough to attend a grade school in a city where I saw first-hand that there are a lot of people who weren't kissed by Lady Luck. They need our help. The beautiful part about Sandy's paper is that the help we provide is not giving a person a fish. It is giving them tools and resources to buy their own net and boat to fish for themselves.

"How, oh Brilliant One, can we perform this miracle?" Great question. The answer is that it will not be miraculous. It will take a decade or more to bear fruit.

I will not dive too heavily into this because it has many nuances. The idea deserves a book that has insight from economists, social leaders, developers, and members of housing authorities. I just want your minds to open to this possibility.

There are a few inventive ways to make this work, but here is a simple idea. Instead of renting, local Public Housing Authorities work with developers to create housing in areas of need or redevelop properties in areas where poverty is common. The Housing Authority then buys the property from contractors. If they buy for less than fair market value, contractors are given tax credits for the difference in sale of fair market less actual sales price. The Housing Authority then fractionalizes ownership and works with residents to create incentive-based programs that ultimately end in the resident **owning** the property. As the resident meets checkpoints, they receive ownership tokens in the property that are used to pay down the mortgage. Children graduate high school? Ownership tokens. You or your children enter a trade union? Ownership tokens. Employment for six consecutive months? Tokens. Level up on your own education? Ownership tokens.

This allows residents to increase their wealth by achieving success without worrying about losing government housing assistance. Homeownership is a major catalyst in wealth accumulation for the average American. For too long, our programs have treated symptoms, not cured poverty. Now we have a chance to incentivize personal and financial growth simultaneously. Not for nothing, as those areas fill with new homeowners incentivized to keep their property values growing, pride in the community grows. A proud community is a safer community because people get more involved in the day-to-day.

This should be a non-partisan issue in every state legislature. This permits the free market to work its witchcraft/magic (depending on where you stand) while permitting residents to live in safe properties without having to decide between paying the rent or electricity this month. It is **crucial** that the housing crisis be fixed, and this is a very powerful tool for our leaders to use.

Cons

This thing isn't all rainbows and unicorns. I started the book by comparing this shift in financial markets to turning a battleship. With new technology comes new friction that slows adoption and change.

For the sake of this book, I will identify four huge pain points to adoption. The first is the glacial speed of legislative changes. The second is the lack of liquidity currently in secondary markets. The final is the lack of transferability between ATS.

Change at the Speed of Government

At the beginning of this book, I mentioned that a major hurdle to this advancement is how slowly governments are adopting technological changes that will permit the formation of a trustless industry.

While almost all states recognize digital signatures as legal forms of intent of a party to be bound by contract terms, that's about the extent of automation that legislators accept. Less than half of the states recognize smart contracts as legal contracts. Some have not even created committees to review blockchain.

What this means to you is that each state will have different regulations surrounding your tokenized offering. Tax law will differ based on state. Heck, you may not even be able to allow certain investors to participate in your offering depending on their domicile. This is most certainly unchartered territory, so you will need to team up with great counsel.

The good news is that there is an enormous groundswell surrounding the digitization of all securities. All involved will have to address the elephant in the room as the leading financial institutions enter the space.

Another ray of hope is that, at the writing of this book, there is a proposal for a 2022 amendment to the Uniform Commercial Code. The UCC, as it is called, governs the contractual obligations in the buying and selling of goods (layman terms). The proposal is being considered to standardize commercial law rules for transactions involving digital assets.[*]

I'm not certain how this will impact the security interests in digitized real estate entities, but it is a good start for the acceptance of digital securities as a means of payment in commerce. If it is adopted, almost all the states will adopt it to create uniformity. Once it is accepted for payment methods and security interests for goods, one could only assume that it will open the door for legislative bodies to consider other digital securities that fall outside the purview of the UCC. Fingers crossed.

New Technology is Expensive

Are you old enough to remember how expensive a personal computer was in the 80s? How about a flat-screen TV? Where have those prices gone as technology improved? You get the point. This con, like the rest in this section, will be obsolete in a few short years.

---

[*] Edwin E. Smith, "The Proposed 2022 Amendments to the Uniform Commercial Code: Digital Assets," Business Law Today from ABA (Business Law Today, March 24, 2022), https://www.businesslawtoday. org/2022/03/proposed-2022-amendments-uniform-commercial-code-digital-assets/.

As for now, however, the cost of tokenizing a property interest and following the necessary steps to remain compliant and in the good graces of the three-letter overlords in our federal government is prohibitive to those with a property valued under $10 million.

How did I come up with that number? I didn't. I've spoken with the people driving the move to tokenization, and this seems to be the best guess value.

Here is a real-world hypothetical. The capital expenditure to tokenize is roughly anywhere from $50,000 to $100,000. When you run your numbers prior to purchasing a property, this will be a line item, just like the cost of new counters and cabinets will be for your kitchen rehabs.

Let's say I bought a 16-unit property for $4 million but will need $1 million for renovations. Depending on the lender, I need to bring at least $1 million to closing. If I decide that I want to tokenize the equity interest in the property, I now have to bring $1.1 million to the deal. That's a 10% increase in the amount that you are bringing out of pocket. Will the increase you drive in rent be worth absorbing that cost?

As the project values and investor contributions increase, it would be worth taking on $50,000–$100k. As we discussed above, providing near-instant liquidity will allow you to drive your cap rate down as you remove the illiquidity premium.

Obviously, this added expense is up to you as an operator. If you want to provide liquidity to yourself as a property owner without dealing with banks, this is a possible option, but it is costly and there are better avenues to provide liquidity. If you have millions brought in by investors to purchase a massive property, then this is definitely a benefit that your investors will appreciate and will be a value driver for your returns.

Illiquidity

"And there it is…" The crushing end to our dream scenario, right? Meh…not so much. **This is a current con**. The trade volume is just not there right now to provide the liquidity one gets in a traditional market or even in crypto. That does not, however, mean there is no liquidity. The option is still there for them to be purchased; your choices are currently limited.

The "option" to be purchased is not exactly a ringing endorsement. I understand that. While it is just a matter of time, I understand the hesitancy. There are a couple of reasons that I feel like money hasn't flocked to secondary markets. The first reason is that most GPs have had the greatest decade of their lives offering deals the traditional way. They have not offered anything exciting in the form of tokenization. The deals that have been listed as tokenized have been few and far between.

The second reason for illiquidity is one that I think will be corrected within the next twenty-four months. That is the problem of lack of education. Too few people understand what we're talking about. Warren Buffet once said something like he didn't invest in things that he didn't understand. This is a prime example of that.

People conflate tokenized securities with Bitcoin and other crypto. They hear blockchain and lose the message as their brain goes into self-defense mode. They hear volatility and corruption, money laundering, and blackmail. They don't hear "backed by real-world assets" and "fully compliant with the SEC."

Overcoming this prejudice is the first obstacle to conquer when educating future market participants. The second is fear of new technology. The idea of this is too complicated for many. Most passive LPs only want to see P&L and what the net operating income is for their investment. They do not want to go to a website and list their tokens or worry about losing them. (Which they will not. The Transfer Agent maintains the ledger. If a private key is lost, they merely are sent a new one by the TA.) They invested in you to take care of everything, just send them the dividend check.

I believe this obstacle will be easier to overcome than you anticipate.

First, I feel like most early adopters will have at least a passing understanding of buying and selling crypto on an exchange. You will just have to fill them in on the difference between investing in marketing hype and a real-world, asset-backed token.

Second, excellent customer service should be one of your primary goals as a GP. You can educate your investors early in the pitch on how this will benefit them. You will bring them comfort with the tech as you ease them into understanding it.

Lack of Transferability

Let's just keep raining on this parade, shall we? I'm kidding. We are about to offer the solution to our problems shortly. This is a temporary con that I believe will die out as the market demands change.

Currently, real estate security tokens are housed on the ATS of individual broker-dealers. You will not find the Aspen token anywhere else besides on tZero, for example. Obviously, this contributes to the lack of liquidity temporarily. To find tokens, you have to hunt for them on a specific website that hosts the ATS.

I'm not 100 percent certain why that is. I think it is due to a desire to control the trade of the tokens and to keep the data centralized. Fewer hands in the cookie jar means less contamination of data.

This way of thinking is short-sighted, in my opinion. The future of tokenized real estate securities is the ability to transfer them among ATS and even crypto exchanges. I mean, you don't just purchase Bitcoin on Coinbase, right? The greater access to market participation a token has, the greater the potential for market participation and liquidity for investors.

The main issue with this currently, is there is no universality of tokens. A large part of this is that it is a compliance trap. It would require the free and transparent exchange of information among multiple broker-dealers. There's a little ego there that needs to be ironed out. Lucky for us, we now have the solution.

The Fix

Universal Asset Tokenization

The solution is an agnostic market solution. One that could ensure "seamless, inter-institutional portability of information governance, risk, and compliance data and records of digital securities and tokenized assets, entities, identities, and transactions."[*]

Now, How Do You Do It?

We have weighed the pros and cons of a digitized offering. The next question becomes, where to start? How do you start? Well, you could try and act as a general contractor and build a team of different service providers to fill each role, or you can find an all-in-one bespoke provider.

---

[*] "Tokenizing Capital Markets," 10XTS, March 31, 2022, https://10xts.com/.

I invested in a company that I have mentioned in this book already. That company is 10XTS, which provides solutions to bring the efficiencies of the new world of decentralized finance to traditional markets. Through contracting with 10XTS, you have access to a network of broker-dealers, transfer agents, and everything else required to make your offering compliant and keep it compliant through its life cycle.

Beyond compliance, 10XTS and its products provide the ability to interact securely and efficiently among institutions, markets, and investors. All of this, and you own your own data. There are no third-party worries. You possess and control the data that your asset and its activities create. They are ahead of the game.

The Why

Pros

Reduction in Legal Risk

Reduction in Stakeholder Risk

Liquidity Premiums

Cutting Out the Administrative Costs

Economic Inclusion

Incentivize Construction of Affordable Housing

Cons

Legislation Woefully Behind the Technology

Upfront Expense

Illiquidity (lack of market and investor education)

Lack of Education in the Market

Lack of Transferability

PART III

THE HOW

XDEX and the Asset Tokenization Lifecycle Process

I want to throw in this disclaimer again. I need to remind you that I have an economic incentive to promote 10XTS. More importantly, I have a duty to promote 10XTS and XDEX because they will play a *major* role in changing the investment world as we know it. All quotations below come from 10xts.com.

XDEX

Multiple parties use multiple information stacks in their own systems, in their own way. The proper transferability of the metadata each party creates and stores is not a sure thing. It is tough to guarantee compliance when you have to translate data from multiple sources. This is where XDEX is your saving grace.

XDEX is 10XTS's flagship product. XDEX is a

> Universal tokenization market infrastructure solution that ensures seamless, inter-institutional portability of information governance, risk, and compliance data and records of digital securities and tokenized assets, entities, identities, and transactions. Securities issuers, investors, custodians, brokers, transfer agents, banks, and regulators must have a comprehensive data solution to define and enforce governance, risk, and compliance across decentralized primary and secondary market infrastructure.

XDEX is the mortar between the bricks of different blockchains and systems that permits your token ecosystem to remain connected and solid against the forces of regulation. It permits traditional markets to fully decentralize.

> XDEX is a fully secure, cloud-native and open API enterprise technology platform and distributed ledger network that standardized the records and metadata to ensure portability and compatibility between institutions — while also providing issuers and their investors with maximum access and control of their information across global, decentralized markets.

XDEX is designed to support modern information requirements that can run parallel to your enterprise systems.

With XDEX, you can achieve better data ownership, governance, risk, and compliance by unifying data from multiple disparate sources into an easily consumable platform that can be securely embedded into smart contracts as an oracle-based solution.

By creating a single repository of all structured and unstructured data from internal and external sources, you can ensure information control and ownership.

A couple of technical points here. API stands for Application Programming Interface. Basically, APIs are like translators that allow different computer applications to communicate together. If you really want to nerd out, Google is your friend.

The second technical point that needs to be addressed is "an oracle-based solution."

An Oracle database is a collection of data treated as a unit. The purpose of a database is to store and retrieve related information. A database server is the key to solving the problems of information management. In general, a server reliably manages a large amount of data in a multiuser environment so that many users can concurrently access the same data. All this is accomplished while delivering high performance. A database server also prevents unauthorized access and provides efficient solutions for failure recovery.

Oracle Database is the first database designed for enterprise grid computing, the most flexible and cost-effective way to manage information and applications. Enterprise grid computing creates large pools of industry-standard, modular storage, and servers. With this architecture, each new system can be rapidly provisioned from the pool of components. There is no need for peak workloads because capacity can be easily added or reallocated from the resource pools as needed.

The database has logical structures and physical structures. Because the physical and logical structures are separate, the physical storage of data can be managed without affecting the access to logical storage structures.[*]

I'm not even going to try and break that down. I just put out the definition on that one. I can, however, break down

____

[*] Introduction to the Oracle Database, May 19, 2022, https://docs.oracle.com/cd/B13789_01/server.101/b10743/intro.htm.

what the passage found on 10XTS.com said regarding what XDEX is as an oracle-based solution.

XDEX is able to communicate efficiently between computer applications, in major part, to the fact that it is agnostic in regard to the creation of the token that you wish to issue. 10XTS has purposely stayed out of the broker-dealer industry to be able to work with all broker-dealers and custodian banks to truly offer a bespoke experience to the issuer and investors. By standardizing records from different sources and data stacks, XDEX permits issuers to offer their tokens across multiple market access points and know that their data is accurately transferred and secured.

Through creating a single collection point of data from multiple sources, you have control of the whole kit and caboodle. The only entity that has the entire collection of your data will be you, and it will be found on XDEX with you as the master of your own domain.

10XTS as Your Primary Tokenization Provider

The previous section explained what XDEX does as your guardian of compliance. I would now like to walk you through the steps of how tokenization works. As you understand the process, the role of XDEX will become clearer, and help you decide if 10XTS is the right choice to guide you through the whole process, from offering to disbursement. If not, stick with trusting XDEX to ensure that you are protected from others' potential malfeasance.

The Asset Tokenization Lifecycle Process™

The Asset Tokenization Lifecycle Process ("ATLP"), besides being a mouthful, is the trademarked IP of 10XTS. It is the roadmap to follow starting with kicking around the idea of tokenizing millions of dollars' worth of real estate and finishing with your multi-million-dollar exit. It will ensure that you stay compliant with authorities and transparent with investors. It will make the process as smooth as it can be at this stage of innovation. Most important, it will allow you and your company to be in full control of your data. You decide who has permission to access it. There is no need for intermediaries unless you want there to be. It gives you full control of your offering and the markets it reaches.

There are three phases of the ATLP. The first phase is the Primary. That is the blood, sweat, and tears phase. It will take you from the structure of your offering entity through the issue of your digitized security. The second is the Secondary phase. That runs the lifecycle after the issue and up to the disposition of your property. The final phase is the Disposition. This is the phase where you clean up after making a killing on the sale of your property.

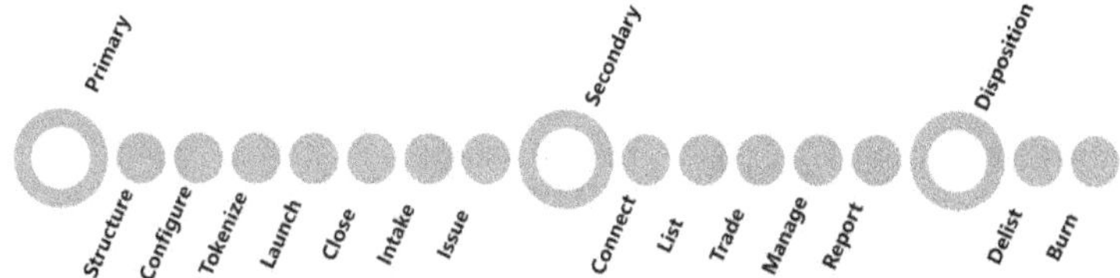

PRIMARY PHASE

The Primary Offering Phase represents the stages of activity that must be undertaken to 1) convert an existing asset to a tokenized format; or, 2) complete the Primary Offering of the asset for sale to the market. Each stage builds on previous stages and is a necessary step to fully completing the initial effort to represent the asset in a token format.

The stages in the Primary Offering Phase are:

1. Structure
2. Configure
3. Tokenize
4. Launch
5. Close
6. Intake
7. Issue

STRUCTURE PHASE

The Structure phase is broken down into two parts. The first part is the Information Governance Structure. The second is the Asset and Offering Structure.

Information Governance Structure

The Structure stage starts with Information Governance Structure, which defines the records management framework for the asset — and, also how the asset relates to transactions between entities. This establishes the foundation for the risk and compliance processes related to conditions and actions comprising the administration of the asset. The Structure phase also defines the Master Data Management (MDM) policy for all information, data, and records pertaining to the asset, offerings, and transactions.

The Information Governance Structure sets a solid foundation, outlining the record management of your asset just as you would when building a house. You are tokenizing interests in your asset for movement in secondary markets. This will require pre-planning as to how the asset will relate to transactions between parties. Processes must be created to manage the risk and compliance of the administration of the asset through its lifecycle. Finally, this phase is where the MDM policy is set in place, so you never have to worry about where information is going as it is recorded.

Don't get me wrong. There is nothing sexy about this part of the process, but it is where you can save yourself millions in future litigation if the concrete and footers are set correctly. To be compliant with the offer of digitized securities through sale, you must have systems in place to properly record each transaction. You must have processes in place to audit your current information. You must have an MDM policy in place so there is continuity across the teams regarding proper information storage surrounding the asset and transactions involving ownership interests in it.

Asset and Offering Structure

Now that the extremely necessary, but ungodly boring part is done, we move to the second step of the Structure stage. This is where you decide the legal entity you will create to own the asset and what type of offering you will use when accepting investors who will ultimately receive the tokenized securities.

> In the next step in the Structure stage, crucial decisions need to be made regarding the terms and conditions of the asset, which correlate to the token. Offering structuring is an integral part of any toke-

nized asset offering, irrespective of the technology employed. Tokenization is not meant to be a way of avoiding compliance with applicable legal and regulatory requirements. Rather, the use of technology is intended to fundamentally improve operational processes to enable innovative financial solutions.

The form and structure of a tokenized asset is crucial in determining the rights and obligations that the investor has in the underlying asset as well as ultimately what form of return they will receive; it will also be the starting point in analyzing how gains and losses on the tokenized security should be taxed. Asset owners and managers should consider the main objectives of the product and the rationale underlying the structure to evaluate how tokenization technology may complement the purpose and enhance utility.

This part will be much easier to grasp for anyone who has ever invested in real estate. Before you ever purchased a property, you created a legal entity, or SPV, that was domiciled in a particular state to control the asset. You did so to shield yourself from liability and to qualify for certain tax breaks offered by the location.

Most of the time, in large projects that make sense to tokenize, you are not paying money out of your own pocket to use as a down payment. You offer interests in your ownership to bring investors in to use their money. The type of offering obviously is very important. Offerings range in cost to your company by the hundreds of thousands of dollars. They come with different holding requirements for investors and reporting requirements for you. Hell, they even have different amounts you can raise.

Before we get going, it is important to make informed legal decisions when contemplating a normal offering. It is even more important when jumping into an offering using innovative technology. The mechanism is still un-settled law. Jurisdictions will vary regarding regulatory frameworks while tax laws could impact the price of the tokenized security and make it less cost-efficient than just doing a traditional offering.

Internally, the offering allows you to dictate when and how returns will be paid. This gives potential investors the abil-ity to compare the risks related to real estate investment with the potential return. It also allows them to calculate what that may look like come tax time. Finally, each type of offering comes with financial pros and cons, with filing costs being prominent.

(I've inserted a recap of the different types of offerings at the end of the book. Again, this is not legal or financial advice. It is merely for convenience, so you don't have to look elsewhere then come back to the book.)

> Compared to traditional issuances, a tokenized asset issuance benefits more from streamlined operations and automated post-issuance corporate action management.

Offering a tokenized interest carries a second layer of consideration when selecting your offering type. A major internal value add of tokenization is to fundamentally improve operational processes to enable the innovative financial solutions that we have discussed. This requires you to define the main objective and rationale of the token to ensure that it complements your goals and enhances utility. The streamlined operations and automated post-issuance corporate action management drive operational costs lower post-issuance, but is it a cost you need to take on? This is the stage where you say yes or no. Once you say yes, you move on to the next stage.

But first, here's one last disclaimer.

> The issuer of tokenized assets must also seek professional advice to make informed decisions about which jurisdictions to include in the structure of the product. The regulatory framework governing tokenized securities will vary between jurisdictions

while the different tax regimes across the jurisdictions could have a significant impact on the price of tokenized assets and its cost-effectiveness. Further, issuers should also seek advice regarding the location of target investors, as this will introduce regulatory considerations related to the marketing and offer of tokenized securities.

In short, as we have discussed, without a uniform regulatory framework to operate under, the impact on your investment from regulation will be localized. Make sure that you get sound counsel from the proper tax and legal folks in your jurisdiction before going any further.

Now, onto the next...

CONFIGURE STAGE

You have contacted your necessary experts and decided that the value of near-instant liquidity to your investors driven by the reduction of risk to them is worth the added cost over a traditional offering. You decide which offering you are going to make and which returns investors may receive. Now, it is time to create the interface that you will use to present the offering to your investors and store asset data.

The Configure stage is where the necessary portals to support the offering and subsequent management are established and built to meet the requirements of the asset. Whether the portals are issuer-owned or third-party, this is the stage where the initial applications and data repositories are defined to support all do the subsequent stages.

If you are like me, you have a rough idea of what a portal is. It can get you into another dimension or time and allow you to either save or destroy civilizations. It is also short for "Data Portals," which are far less interesting to discuss unless you are trying to give your investors the best experience they can receive.

Data portals, in a basic sense, are unique websites that often contain lots of information and data, kind of a library of sorts.[**]

Your tokenized offering will require more than one portal. The total number depends on whether you own the asset already and are tokenizing an existing interest or are planning on tokenizing from the jump. This is true if your

---

[**] Greg Rossi, "What Is a Data Portal? Everything Explained," Zuar, February 22, 2022, https://www.zuar.com/blog/what-is-a-data-portal-everything-explained/.

company is going to create the portal or whether a third party will maintain it.

If you are planning on tokenizing your offering from the jump, one of the first portals that will be created is the Primary Offering Portal. There is no real mystery what this portal is created for. This portal will be where your investors go to review and subscribe to your amazing offer. It will also manage their experience, and provide the necessary KYC/AML identity verifications, accredited investor status checks, subscription documents signatory, payment facilitation, and any other investor-facing activities. This portal will maintain the basis of your relationship and help define your fiduciary duties, kind of like a website for your wedding video and vows.

If you are just renewing your vows...terrible analogy here, sorry, and tokenizing an existing property, you do not need to create this portal.

Regardless of whether the asset is new or old, a good CEO or GP will want to provide investors with ease of access to important information regarding their investment and access to trade their ownership interest. Through the creation of a Records Management/Investor Communication portal, you can do just that. An Investor Communication portal allows you to provide your investors with news and communications as well as investor services. You will be able to link your offering to secondary markets here, giving investors access to the market without requiring them to go on a Google wild goose chase.

Further, this is where you will store important information. Items such as individual investor accounts and necessary related documents will be stored here, as well as fiduciary custody connectivity. This portal is the go-to holder for records management and information governance.

If done correctly, this information can be linked to accounts and wallets held by investors while also connecting with third-party service providers so transfer agents, fiduciary custody management, exchanges, and ATS trading to provide a comprehensive recording of all activities revolving around the asset.

Finally, depending on your offering and your location, you may have to use a transfer agent. You will need to have a transfer agent portal. Here, the official system of record of ownership of the asset will be maintained. This portal allows the transfer agent to maintain the book of entry of shareholders and a ledger of their activity.

TOKENIZE STAGE

Ladies and Gentlemen, the moment that you have all been waiting for...almost. Tokenizing the ownership interest of the asset.

> The Tokenize stage is where blockchain tokens are created to represent the units of account bound to the security interest of the asset.

This is the stage where you create a cool name for your token and divvy up the tokens to represent each investor's position in the SPV. This is the part that seems the most like a cryptocurrency, but it is not. Remember, this is a direct digital representation of ownership of a real-world asset, not a speculative string of binary numbers.

> The token and how it is bound to the security itself becomes subject to jurisdictional regulation and compliance. Because of the variation in laws and requirements, this may be simple or can be more complex.

The location of the asset and the location of the investor will dictate how your locale views your ownership interest in the asset merely by holding tokens. This was a huge con in our "Cons" section of the "Why?" part. This technology and financial application is so new that many jurisdictions have not passed legislation to recognize certain layers of blockchain as good enough to provide proper control for security. For example, here in the good ole US of A, a Layer One public blockchain doesn't pass the muster.

Why? Well, a Layer One is the public blockchain and it is the first layer in a decentralized ecosystem. Remember, the purpose of using blockchain is to domicile data in an immutable and decentralized network so that there is no main point of storage, making it safer from attack. The benefit of Layer One is it allows the network to scale, or smoothly grow as more data is attached to the chain. The concern with scaling is that current technology does not allow blockchain to scale quickly, optimize security, and maintain decentralization at the same time. At best, two out of three properties of blockchain will not be compromised, while the third will be lacking. The founder of Ethereum, Vitalik Buterin, called this the "scalability trilemma."

The beauty of real estate tokenization and trading is that trading will happen at a comparatively slower rate, permitting a slower scale. Most people invest in real estate knowing that value rarely increases overnight. As a result, security and decentralization will be optimized. That, however, is not sufficient yet.

Therefore, a Layer Two chain is necessary to meet U.S. securities control standards. A Layer Two chain is built on top of the existing blockchain that you are using to tokenize your asset. That was almost easy to understand (sarcasm). A Layer Two chain allows blockchain activities to take place independently of the Layer One public blockchain. For our purpose, an issuer or a transfer agent provides the necessary control to appease the taskmasters of the U.S. regulatory bodies. As a result, a Layer Two chain will be created to maintain the ledger of the transfer agent to act as the book-entry system where they can track investors and ownership independent of the public blockchain.

In English, Layer One will show the world the records of security interests. Layer Two will hold the records of who owns what and when.

Okay, all of that word salad to let you know that,

> Tokens can be created on the Layer Two chain to represent the unit of account and tracking method at the issuer or the transfer agent level. Those tokens are held in the issuer's account to represent treasury until such time they are issued to investors by moving those tracking took entry tokes to the respective account and wallet at the investor level.

Basically, the tokens are created at the layer that the U.S. deems worthy. They are held in escrow, so to speak, until the

Issue Stage when the tokens are sent to investors' wallets. (If you do not know what a wallet is, please research it. It is extremely important.)

LAUNCH PHASE

This is the "rubbing elbows" phase — PR and marketing, digital ads, and legal hand wringing. Remember, this phase will be influenced by the type of offering you chose and your locale. You may not be able to advertise; you may not be able to show your sweet property to people in specific countries. It is extremely important that you have good counsel heading into this phase. You obviously want to reach the maximum number of people you are legally permitted to reach, but maximum *plus one* could be legal suicide.

If you already have the entity created and property owned and are only looking to tokenize existing ownership interest, you will not need to go through the launch phase.

> Launch phase is where the primary offering campaign is initiated to include marketing and promotion of the offer to invest. This can be brokered under properly licensed third-party efforts, or under the appropriate exemptions or registrations, can be conducted directly by the issuer.

As I said before, this is where those able to know about the investment, get to know. You can offer it yourself, or you can outsource it. **Just stay inside the lines.** This isn't legal advice; this is common sense.

Generally, the campaign leverages the Primary Offering portal and, in the instance of online marketing, drives investors to the location to register and complete the subscription process.

Obviously, you want your portal to be as user-friendly as possible, and here is where that pays off. You are grabbing their attention while making it easy to register and fill out all the necessary legal crap to participate in your offering. They'll get to see why you spent $15,000 for an attorney to draft that perfect Private Placement Memorandum.

CLOSE PHASE

Another stage that you don't have to worry about if you are tokenizing an existing asset is the Close stage. Close refers to wrapping up the launch and making sure that you are right with the Lord...or at least the powers that be.

Upon completion of the Primary Offering, the Close stage is where the final activities are conducted to end the process. This may involve breaking escrow and taking receipt of the proceeds of the offering and any other filings that may be required such as state blue sky law exemptions.

This is straightforward. If your offering is subject to blue sky laws, get the forms completed here. You are paying for the property at this stage as well. The funds you raised are now going to go towards whatever financial requirements your lender has to qualify for the mortgage. There is not much more to be said here than "Congrats on increasing your net worth, unless you bought at a bad price, then you are in trouble!" (Joking...)

INTAKE PHASE

The Intake phase is the part that scares the hell out of traditionalists, particularly anyone who is a career paper pusher. This phase is where all the information that is usually stored in a filing cabinet or server is stored and encrypted. Voter rights and dividend payments can be pro-grammed to be automated via smart contracts. Efficiency and accuracy are King.

The Intake stage is where information traditionally stored in paper or document form is uploaded to the blockchain and encoded into encrypted has values.

Thus, we are transforming the body of recordation and evidence to hash-based metadata.

In this phase, all the necessary documents, traditionally paper or computer, are uploaded to the Layer Two blockchain. Proof of ownership and any other real-world documents are magically turned into "hash-based metadata," or encrypted and encoded data about data. In this case, metadata is data that refers to the documents required to show ownership interest in the asset and peg the value token to the actual ownership value of the asset.

The Intake Phase is also where workflows are developed and even automated with secure logging to meet governance, risk, and compliance policies.

The Intake phase is where tedious management and investor-related processes can be streamlined and automated to ensure efficient recording and transfer of important data between stakeholders.

Encoding the body of recordation helps to streamline processes by allowing separate stakeholders to have secure access to the same copy of data, which cannot be altered without validation from other stakeholders.

This sentence perfectly describes what makes the use of blockchain so powerful. You don't need the trust of the people in your network. Sounds counter-intuitive, but it is a fundamental strength. If information regarding your asset, your investment, can't be altered by a back-stabbing partner or another party, then you have security in the knowledge that you are where your numbers say you are. In order to change data, the other stakeholders on the network must give the okay, or be in consensus for the dorks out there. The explanation goes a bit further.

> Immutable transaction records enable a high degree of automation to deliver much-needed process optimization and efficiency to investments. Other actions that are programmable throughout the investment lifecycle include investor and corporate action management, such as distributing dividends and shareholder's votes, which are covered under the Manage phase.

We will dive into this a bit deeper in the Manage phase, but the fact that records can't be screwed with allows each stakeholder to have confidence that the information pertaining to the asset is accurate. It allows authorities to have that same confidence and trust.

While the lack of trust needed is a great thing to weirdly create a strong quasi-trust in the stakeholders (I mean, it will be very difficult to get screwed over), it also makes the operation of the management of the investment cheaper.

Dividends will be programmed through smart contracts and automatically released (Remember, we covered smart contracts in the WHY part of the book). Voting will be recorded with confidence that all votes could not be tampered with. This is all possible due to the nature of blockchain.

> Technology enables fractional ownership to be securely managed as a digital record, investor due diligence and compliance protocols to be automated, and transactional settlement to be completed digitally. The cumulative effect of these changes is to significantly reduce the time and economic costs associated with trading previously illiquid assets, which benefits asset owners and investors alike through unlocked liquidity. As regulatory regimes across the globe evolve to meet these technological developments, secondary market trading for tokenized assets will continue to grow and thrive.

As we discussed in the "Why" part, real estate investing comes with a lot of pain points, but the most prominent is lack of liquidity. Your money just stares at you from the other side of the portal, and you can't do anything about it without wrecking a legal entity or involving a bank and/or lawyers. By tokenizing your asset and listing it on secondary markets, you remedy that pain. You take away the inflammation and reduce the swelling. Your investors will thank you. All of this is possible because of the efficiency of data recording on an immutable chain using smart contracts to instantly settle transactions whose settlements can't be edited. Quick and easy.

ISSUE PHASE

This is the most time-demanding phase from a customer services perspective. There are going to be 1,000 emails, calls, and questions regarding "How in the hell do I get my tokens into my wallet?" You can have the greatest roadmap ever, but this part is unavoidable during this early stage of adoption. Just be prepared with a smile, otherwise you'll pull your hair out.

> The Issue phase is the process where book entry asset tokens are distributed to owner accounts and wallets on a network. Unless the tokenization process is being conducted for a legacy asset, the issuance process likely involves a primary offering as discussed in the Launch and Close stages.

This is the moment that your investors have all been waiting for. They now receive the tokens they gave you capital for. It reflects their security interest in your investment, and depending on the offering you chose, may provide them with the ability to cash out right away if your management skills appear to be subpar. Or...if the hype of the area increases the value of your asset, they can cash out and not cost themselves money contacting attorneys. It is all at their fingertips.

> During the securities offering, investors purchase the security interests, and the investors' information is recorded on the digital record of security holders, members, or stakeholders.

> Issuance of the security tokens to accounts can take place when all the business, legal, and regulatory components are in place, satisfying the requirements in the Structure phase with the asset being defined, parameterized, and bound over to a custodian who maintains independent audit and controls with all of the legal documentation and enumerations completed in the Structure phase.

This is where Layer Two comes into play. Once you have made your bed, and all loose ends are tied to ensure compliance, the tokens can be sent to your investors. The independent transfer agent records all investor info regarding units received and maintains a record of the contracts made between the company and investment to ensure audit capabilities that are uncompromised as trades begin.

SECONDARY PHASE

The Secondary Phase includes all of the stages necessary to enable and facilitate secondary market listing, trading, management and reporting of the asset as it moves through the secondary markets.

What good is all this time, effort, and capital expenditure to create tokens if you don't have a place to redeem their value? I have harped on the benefits of the trustless relationship that stakeholders can peacefully maintain due to immutable record-keeping. That, however, isn't all that exciting to your investors. What they want is a return, one way or the other. That is what the Secondary Phase facilitates.

CONNECT PHASE

The first action of the Secondary Phase is the Connect phase. This is where your guru meets with the gurus from the ATS or secondary market to create a connection between your blockchain and their trading ecosystem. This is, in short, all about proper connection.

The connect phase is where the previous efforts are connected to external business and data ecosystems — usually via some form of API-based services middle layer. Examples are fiduciary custodians and exchanges or Alternative Trading Systems (ATS).

API stands for Application Programming Interface. Its role is to play communicator between two applications. There is information on your public blockchain that the exchange or ATS requires to be able to list and permit the trade of your token while staying compliant. Do not ask me to explain it further, because I can't. I'm only a man, not a machine (Rocky IV reference if you are old enough to get it.) I'm joking, again. I'll get any answers you need.

This is an extremely important phase. An exchange, I'd hope, would not list your token until all the bugs are worked out with the API so that all trades completed on the exchange are accurately recorded in your blockchain, and the Layer Two chain is responsible for audit processes. Nobody wants to be responsible for a $1,000,000 purchase of tokens that are not recorded properly as a very simple example of what could go wrong.

The Connect phase usually involves a level of custom enterprise software integrations between organizations, that establish, agree, and comply with the common metadata structures defined in the Configure stage.

Your blockchain host will need to work closely with the ATS or exchange to customize the communication between your Layer Two custodian, transfer agent, your Layer One blockchain, and the application that you wish to use to trade your tokens.

> If not previously created, this is also the phase where public blockchain network smart contracts are developed to consume the information, governance, risk, and compliance metadata developed during the Build phase.

If you wait to build your smart contracts to mesh with the application you are going to trade on, this is the time to do it. There's no reason to go through the expense and effort to create Layer One smart contracts and tokens until the security is going to list and trade. Tokenization takes place as book entry, but due to the additional lift for secondary transfer, may be sufficient until the 144(a) restriction on secondary trading is lifted. Most of the industry is focused on creating the Layer One out of the gate, but it's an exercise in selling people the buzzword while there's no reason to do it just yet.

LIST PHASE

When I used to think of the List phase, I thought of the culmination of the hype party. The Offering phase is where the real schmoozing is. That is where we push the potential positives of our assets and sweet talk our way into what used to be checkbooks. Now I guess they are crypto wallets, wire transfers...whatever object and process that will eventually put capital in our investment. Good times, good PR, and good marketing are combined to drum up awareness of the ability to participate in an ownership interest. The same is kind of true in the List phase.

If you have any experience using Coinbase, Gemini, or any other exchange, you will notice that their offerings continually grow, much like the Nasdaq. You have noticed that a lot of tokens that you have never heard of appear, then a few take off like rockets, and investors see 1,500 percent returns in two months. You have also seen a few that lost 99 percent of their value right when they were listed or made available for sale because the original investors flooded the market as soon as they could.

The good news for us is that our tokens won't trade on hype. Unlike tokens released without any program or plan to support their value, our tokens will trade on value generated by the operations of the asset. As you saw in the

Aspen token example, it is very easy to gauge the value of your token over time by merely finding the Net Operating Income of your asset, the cap rate of your asset's location, and doing some math from there.

What is really important in this phase for us is not promoting the listing with pizzaz but meeting the compliance standards of the network that is going to permit us to list with them. This is a major purpose of XDEX.

> List stage is where the security and respective token is registered and listed for trading on a licensed exchange, Alternative Trading System (ATS), or broker-dealer network for secondary transactions between investors who wish to buy and sell the asset for investment purposes.

This is the stage where you select that awesome name for your token, give it a sweet trade symbol, and give your investors access to secondary market liquidity in the event they need to sell. Again, if you want a visual of what this looks like, tZero's listing of the Aspen token is a great example. It looks just like any other traditional security listing on any traditional exchange.

Selecting the proper exchange or ATS is your decision and yours alone. It will come down to the value/cost analysis of trade volumes and liquidity versus how much they charge you. Just like purchasing the asset in the first place, you can't make up for a bad deal on the back end.

> Listing usually involves contracting the trading venue and meeting compliance with their reviews of the principles, the entity, and the security instrument.

If you're into the crypto world news, you will know that the laws and regulations that exchanges and ATS have to operate under are not settled. Further, the currency that they facilitate the trading of is constantly the target of regulatory rumors. As a result, they must dot each "I" and cross each "T" and then double-check those marks to ensure they are completed lest they come into the crosshairs of the regulators.

I'm a University of Kentucky basketball fan, so this seems like an adept analogy even if you don't like it. When John Calipari was hired, he came with the baggage of being partly responsible for getting two programs placed on probation. The University of Kentucky men's basketball program does not have a squeaky-clean image either. They've had a gambling scandal as well as a recruiting scandal in their past. In fact, one of my earliest memories of them was how bad they were in 1989 because they were placed on probation, lost a ton of talent, and lost scholarships so they couldn't replace the transfers. Anyway, the combination of the two put them firmly in the spotlight and under the microscope of the NCAA. Both parties had to ensure compliance with the letter of the law or face the wrath of Khan. That is what I envision crypto exchanges and ATS face when they take on tokens.

> Investors seeking trading privileges on the exchange will require individual investor account applications, as well as KYC/AML identity verifications. Ideally, those processes and their respective documentation would also be ingested and associated with their account information at the cap table level with the issuer or the transfer agent.

"Know Your Customer" and "Anti-Money Laundering" (you see the KYC/AML in there?) are mandatory processes a company is required to undertake to ensure that they know who is investing in their company. Lucky for us, we've created a Layer Two blockchain where the transfer agent recorded all this info as investors signed to participate in the offering.

> With many forms of security registration, the use of a transfer agent is required, which means the custodian

and exchange must be able to seamlessly communicate trade and investor information to update the shareholder registry and cap table.

Again, at the time of your offering, you met with your attorney and whoever else to go over all the requirements that you would need to meet to present a compliant offering. You knew what was being asked of you prior to making it to this point in the process. The Layer Two blockchain is up and running. The API was created during the Connect phase for seamless communication.

TRADE PHASE

For the life of your offering, you have spouted the phrase "near-instant liquidity." Like some sort of FinTech evangelist, you have eased the fears of your congregation by promising to ease their pain points. "Alleluia, I say to you, 'Illiquidity be thy illness, Liquidity be thine medicine.'"

This is where the value of tokenization in enhancing liquidity is realized, in efficient secondary market trading.

You, your team, and 10XTS have completed the hard work of getting to this point. Now your promises become a reality. Your investors, **and you,** can now reclaim your initial investment if that is what they, or you, want to do. I'm just going to tell you this right here and now, this is another stage where your customer relation skills will be tested. Just as in the Issue phase, the use of a new technology and method of doing things is going to trigger hundreds of emails, texts, phone calls, smoke signals...whatever. Make sure you have covered yourself with the help that you will need to address all concerns in a timely manner. It seems like common sense, but proper customer service has gone the way of the dinosaurs recently. This is an easy place to build trust and word of mouth.

> The information governance, risk, and compliance framework becomes the chassis to connect a common data set across the decentralized capital markets industry value chain.

The Structure phase, of all the phases in the ATLP, took the longest to complete. Remember, it set the foundation for sending data into the proper locations in your network. That data was organized according to its role. Was it information regarding governance? Risk? And/or compliance?

As tokens are traded, and tracing ownership and investor information becomes more complex, having confidence in your recording protocols is paramount. That is why you and 10XTS spent so much time preparing your structure.

You can have confidence that a token that traded on ATS 1 will not be able to be traded on Exchange 2 by the former owner, that dirty bastard.

> Offering sponsors and issuers can enable trading of their asset across the spectrum of trading and trade enablement platforms — over-the-counter arrangements, third-party exchanges, or even dark pool private equity.

Just because you have permitted trading of the security interest in the asset that you manage does not mean you must list it everywhere. Remember, currently, security tokens are only listed on one ATS or exchange anyway. The "universal token" that you created gives you the flexibility to list and trade wherever it makes the most sense for you and your asset.

> The post-trade settlement process is optimized through the information automation and authorizations between entities and individuals.

As we just mentioned, the worst thing that can happen to our security interests is that the chain of custody of a token is broken. If I can't trace Hash 1 from the original investor through the life of the token, then I can't settle with my investor correctly. Obviously, litigation would follow.

Currently, a real-world example of a nightmare scenario is playing out. Most everyone remembers the price drive of Gamestop ("GME") shares. It was driven by Reddit members banding together to stick it to the Man. I'm not an investment guru, so I can't explain long/short positions, but basically, they were trying to screw hedge funds out of their short position on the GME shares. In doing so, supposedly billions would be lost by the funds.

Through the power of the interwebz, Reddit users began buying shares of GME on the trading app Robinhood, a broker-dealer. Like moths to the flame, more and more came, and the price skyrocketed (as of March 2022, the current 52-week high was $348.50). This detonated short positions. It also exposed some significant flaws in how trading currently is recorded and permitted.

When you buy a share through a brokerage currently, you **do not own** that share. I was "today years old" when I learned that nifty little fact. Cede & Co. put your name on a ledger, give some sort of legal ownership rights, but never will your name be registered as the owner.

Why does that matter? I'm not going to go through the entire machination. I'm citing this article in the footnotes for this little blurb. Please read about it there because a lot of shady things went down, albeit legally shady.[***]

What I will say is that due to the current setup, more shares were able to be sold than were in existence. Why is that? Because brokers lend shares that you *think* you own to others holding positions and charge interest. Pretty crazy shit. So, there are not actually more shares in circulation, there were just two parties with the rights to one share.

When investors got sick of it and changed brokers, their accounts' cost per share basis was higher than their contracted price. Why? The answer is legal price manipulation. Research Dark Pools and their impact on the true value of the share that you thought you owned.

I don't know if you found this relevant or not, but I did. Having the ability to transparently trace ownership through a decentralized network ledger is a major advantage in investor trust compared to the smoke and mirrors currently in play at brokerages. (Going further, the math to find the value of a security interest in a real estate asset

____

*** Jack Tazman, "GameStop and the Great Direct Registration Experiment," Upside Chronicles, January 13, 2022, https://upsidechronicles. com/2021/
12/11/gamestop-and-the-great-direct-registration-experiment/.

is orders of magnitude easier than trying to find the true value of your share in Amazon.)

Remember, the whole point of tokenizing security interests in your asset is to address pain points in real estate investing, not create more.

MANAGE PHASE

The manage phase is a **major** value driver. I hang out with mostly value-add investors. They purchase commercial residential or commercial properties that have operating inefficiencies, i.e., terrible management, and they fix them. Often times, they improve the facilities to meet current market conditions. They will put systems in place to generate more income, and they will reduce costs in other areas. Rents increase and losses decrease. At the end of the day, they will have a more appealing asset on the outside and a higher net operating income on their ledger. As you know, the value of their asset just increased.

After the improvements, it is imperative that a good management company run the property to ensure that all those improvements were not in vain. Proper management will allow the owner to make real-time assessments of their asset and ensure that value continues to rise.

Post-tokenization management will continue throughout the life of the token until maturity or redemption and disposal.

Like the great property manager that drives value through efficient operations, 10XTS will ensure that the recordation and governance of your token will add value to your asset. Each transaction will be recorded on XDEX and on the independent Layer Two chain through the APIs created by 10XTS to pull and push data with third-party ATS and exchanges.

In post-tokenization management, automated corporate action management processes, including dividend distribution and shareholder voting, can be enforced with business rules and smart contracts. Issuers retain control over the final approval or rejection of investors who pass automation restrictions before transfers are finalized.

There are those smart contracts again. Their role cannot be downplayed. They are the bedrock for trustless transactions. Automating administrative processes within the confines of the rules and roles laid out in your PPM saves massive amounts of time. Time is money. However, it is not just a blind disbursement of funds or blind voting forms going out to your investors. You remain in control of your data and the functions that your data performs.

> Every transaction throughout the life of a token is recorded immutably on a blockchain.

We really don't need to rehash this again. Once that block is hashed, it is not trifled with unless a consensus of stakeholders agrees that information can be changed.

> The administration of the asset includes every form of reporting to meet internal and external governance, risk, compliance directed requirements.

The SEC, IRS, and other three-letter pythons around the neck of the free-market enterprise will require that you can trace your transactions. As funds flow in and out, the complexity of tracing the ownership interests in the asset grows. If at any time, one of those bad boys requests information, such as an audit, you will have that data ready at the push of a button. This is one of the greatest value adds a business can have.

REPORT STAGE

Ah, those pesky three-letter agencies. They always want information when they want it. They set standards that must be met, lest you pay out in fines and penalties.

As the trading and management activity ensues, invariably there are many forms of reporting requirements that must be met. Whether it's reporting to investors by the issuer, or reporting by licensed intermediaries to the regulators because all transactional data is captured and stored on chain, it is a matter of aggregating the information, filtering and sorting, and presenting the information in a format necessary for use.

With the appropriate application interfaces, reporting can be reduced from weeks, days, even hours, to a single click as the authorized administrator can provision the information and give permission to the export to any external party.

Okay, it isn't just the government that will require reporting. Your investors will as well. XDEX makes this a snap. All the data that is captured through trades, day-to-day operation of the asset, whatever can be easily grouped, sorted, and presented in any manner required by the authorities or your stakeholders. We're talking in a matter of seconds. Think about all the overhead and effort you save!

Reporting is no longer an annual or quarterly event. With the right configuration, reporting can become a near real-time function, providing unprecedented access to broad data sets.

Real-time info given to those who need it at the click of a button whenever it is needed, gotta love technological advances.

DISPOSITION PHASE

At the end of the asset's lifecycle, the Disposition phase is the final list of activities to terminate the asset's digital information and data record existence.

These are the rules and workflow processes to ensure an orderly and compliant shutdown of the body of recordation.

For example, at the maturity of a limited partnership fund, there is a final disbursement of assets and dissolution of the entity. Traditional recordkeeping principles and requirements continue to apply any digital records before depreciation.

A very important aspect of this type of offering to remember is that tokenization and trading the tokens on a secondary market are added benefits of investing in your asset. The owners of interests at the close of the property (hopefully a very profitable sale) will still be paid out in a traditional method. The Disposition phase of the tokens merely pulls the tokens from exchanges and other ATS. You will still need to make your investors whole in the same method that you would with any other close.

DELIST PHASE

Should the asset be listed on secondary markets, the Delist stage is where the process to remove the asset from each of the markets is undertaken. Each trading venue will maintain its own processes and requirements to remove the asset from their active listing.

Depending on who created your token and who permitted the listing on their exchange or ATS, the means of delisting your token will vary. Obviously, you will know this prior to applying to list, but it is something to keep in mind. It is an added cost.

All documentation pertaining to the proper processes should also be captured and retained by the issuer to maintain a full scope of records.

This is where the new mixes with the old. As settlement takes place and after, it is extremely important that Layer Two, in our case XDEX, maintains the ledger of interest holders for any required tax and verification processes that may be needed for the following tax year.

BURN PHASE

> Burn stage is where all the publicly exchangeable forms of tokens are removed from circulation, locked, and/or destroyed from further movement throughout any market ecosystem.

All assets have some end date, whether it's because of acquisition or the expiration of a fund time horizon. Because blockchain tokens are immutable, there still must be a phase where the asset is disengaged from the network to parallel what happens to it in the real world.

> The book entry ledger of the final snapshot of the cap-stack should be retained, as well as any and all records pursuant to retention policies and laws required for regulatory supervision.

That's it. All the process right there. The Asset Tokenization Lifecycle Process takes your offering from idea to reality to close. It is the process that permits your investors to move their interests freely without destroying the legal entity you created. You save yourself thousands in legal fees while providing a service that your competitors are unable to match.

Going further, this new means of real estate investment has the potential to fundamentally change the real estate industry forever. The ability to lessen the risk of illiquidity not only benefits investors, but it allows you to compress cap rates by limiting the illiquidity premium currently necessary in today's offerings.

Even better, this opens a new world of economic inclusion that is closed to anyone not considered, at best, a sophisticated investor. People who have not been able to benefit from the safe-ish returns of real estate investing and the tax breaks that come with owning a property can now participate. People will no longer be shut out because they can't afford a $50,000 buy-in. They will be able to create their own portfolio of properties by adding fractions of ownership with every paycheck. Heck, we even discussed how it will help people afford their own homes and begin the journey to economic independence. All of this is possible due to the technology of tokenizing interests in an SPV and the trustless, immutable nature of processes driven by and reported in a blockchain database. See, not all tech companies are evil!

I hope that this book gives you the ground-level knowledge that will help you feel confident in understanding the buzzwords and ideas behind the tokenization of security interests in your future offerings. The world of traditional markets is changing, and I trust that this book will help you get five steps ahead of your competition.

If you have any questions, feel free to contact me. If I don't have the answer, I have the resources to find it for you. This is my future and yours. Let's build wealth together and bring the rest of the country along for the ride.

Kyle Stevie
steviepropertiesllc@gmail.com
513-623-4326

APPENDIX

SEC Filing

The "easiest" way to avoid any guessing on whether an offering is exempt or not is to just say, "Screw it," and register the offering with the SEC and go all corporate big dog with an Initial Public Offering ("IPO"). I hope that the quotes around the word *easiest* in the previous sentence accurately represent my sarcasm. I could not lay it on thicker. Very little is easy about registering a security offering with the SEC. (Remember, you are offering a security interest in your property when you bring an investor on who will anticipate returns while providing zero labor.) To hammer my point home further, carve out some leisure time. Grab a cool beverage, and treat yourself to the blissful, light reading of the Securities Act of 1933 and the Exchange Act of 1934. If you cannot get enough of the securities genre, you can also search some accompanying Federal rules, court interpretations, and your state's regulations.

The first difficulty comes in drafting your documents to file with the SEC. Unless you are a lawyer who practices in the field of Securities, I would not recommend doing it on your own. (What's the saying, "The man who represents himself has a fool for a client?") That means, dun dun dun, that you will have to hire an attorney. *Yeah!!!* It is a sunk cost; it is unavoidable, but it can save your bacon. Choose wisely. If you do not, you will be paying for an attorney twice, if you get what I'm saying.

Anyway, attorneys worth hiring to help draft your offering are not cheap. This is not exactly the area to skimp on. That means you are potentially staring down the pricing barrel of a $450 an hour and up gauged bullet. An IPO filing could require preparation of *thousands* of pages of documentation. (You get why they can charge $450 an hour now. Who wants to write thousands of pages of anything? I'm winded right now, and I'm on, like, page 10.) I am not the best mathematician, but thousands of pages at $450/hour is staggering. Side Note: most pages will be boilerplate, which saves some time and money...but still.

All told, you are looking at hundreds of thousands of dollars. Why sink that much money into a project if you do not have to?

Exempt Offerings

For all the flack it receives, the SEC is not completely controlled by heartless money-grubbers who care only about the "Big Boys." Just mostly...I'm kidding...a little. In 1982, Congress decided that the cost to list a public company was too prohibitive for many companies. It stifled their growth as they could not raise the funds necessary to gain traction or even get started. Exemptions were carved out to permit companies to offer equity in exchange for capital. For the sake of time, efficiency, and your sanity, we will only focus on a few exemptions. As an added layer of protection, where your project could have multiple offerings, you will want to verse yourself in Rule 152 and, again, contact your attorney to make sure that multiple offerings meet the standards of the Integration Doctrine laid out there. Finally, exempted offerings have specific rules regarding solicitations, participants, exit times, and capital raises that are yet further reasons to have an attorney to bounce ideas off of.

REGULATION D EXEMPTIONS

While Vitamin D is a major building block of your immune system, happiness, energy, and pretty much all good things in life, Regulation D (Reg D) is your offering equivalent.

You're welcome for the analogy. Reg D, as the cool kids call it, houses rules 504, 505, and 506. These rules are among the most used exemptions from the Securities Act of 1933. Just remember, some of these are subject to state registration and qualifications. So, your offering is exempt at the Federal level, but your state still wants to hear all about it.

Why would your company want to offer securities under Regulation D and not other exemptions? Well, my friend, here are a few benefits of this exemption. First, and this goes with all Reg D offerings, the costs associated with a D offering are dramatically lower than offering a publicly registered security. While discussing the big picture cost, a specific line item is the underwriting costs associated with an IPO and D offering. IPO underwriters charge a commission of up to 13 percent of the proceeds of the sale of the securities. Compare that to 3 percent for underwriting a D offering. Additionally, you can keep your company's confidential information a little more secure since you will not have to provide as much information. Finally, you will be able to complete the creation and execution of the security sale much more quickly and efficiently.

There are three types of offerings that fall under Reg D that we will discuss in this section of the book. What you are about to read is extremely broad and condensed for time. I suggest that you read these in full on your own. They each have their own rules regarding solicitation, offering size, investor type, and whether they are preempted from state laws (that is, even though I'm exempt from the FED, I still have to be cool with the state.) The first rule that we will discuss is Rule 504, followed by 505, and, wait for it....506. To throw a wrench in the pattern, we will discuss Rule 506(b) and 506(c) because they are the same but very, very different. Let's get started.

RULE 504 OF REG D

Rule 504 permits you to raise quite a bit of money. If you so choose, you could raise up to $10,000,000, less the aggregate offering price for all securities sold within the twelve months before the start of and during the offering of securities. That is a fancy way of saying, "If you raise money in January and then again in December, you better not raise more than a total of $10,000,000 between them. If so, it is your ass."

Now, you may be thinking: *Fantastic, I raise $10 mil, close on my deal, and let my investors get their money back and then some by selling their shares. That's the purpose of the book, I get it, and I'm ready to rock.* Rule 504 requires restricted securities. That means that your investors will not be able to transfer their shares for twelve months. If you provide liquidity before that, you will need to jump through the hoops of registering, .and nobody wants that (as we've seen). Well, kind of. There are exceptions here to the exemption. It is based on your state's security laws. Talk to your attorney, Yo.

We know the monetary limits we can offer and how long it will be before investors can cash out, but who can we offer them to, and how do we reach them? Rule 504 of Reg D allows general solicitation in limited circumstances. Talk to your attorney and use their advice to know how you can offer your investment opportunity and to whom. The good news is there are no investor requirements to be met, and you just need to fill out a Form D to file your offering. Just note that you have **fifteen** days to file the Form D after the **first** sale of the securities.

I generally try to see the good in everyone, but the SEC does not. Your 504 offering will be disqualified if you trip the "bad actor" provisions of Rule 506(d). The "bad actor" disqualification provision states, very broadly, that basically, if any managing member of your company, anyone helping to issue your securities, or any of your security holders own over 20 percent of the voting equity securities, your security will not be exempt if they acted badly in the past. If that person or persons had been shady and was convicted of a felony or misdemeanor in regard to a securities fraud in the last ten years, your security offering is not exempt, and you will have to register with the SEC. There are a whole host of other reasons that your compatriot is an awful human and will wreck your offering. You can find all of them through the footnoted source.* Again, and you guessed it, consult that fine counsel we keep hyping up.

You have done your part. You have vetted your "covered people," and they are beacons of all that is good in our Capitalistic society.

RULE 506 OF REG D

When I started making myself a nuisance in investor groups, particularly those that centered around real estate syndications, I kept seeing offerings touted as "506..." offerings. Naturally, that piqued my interest. *What is Rule 506?* Well, Rule 506 creates an exemption for limited offers and sales without regard to the dollar amount of offering. Now, why were all these GPs using this form of offering to get off the SEC's radar? The answer to that question goes a bit deeper.

---

* "Other," SEC Emblem, July 14, 2017, https://www.sec.gov/info/smallbus/secg/bad-actor-small-entity-compliance-guide.htm.

There is an assortment of benefits to a Rule 506 offering. Depending on which exemption you use, you may be able to broadly solicit and generally advertise your offering, increasing its visibility and investor interest. You could offer to non-accredited investors. A major benefit is that this style of offering is **not** subject to state registration or qualification. Less paperwork and less money going into the hands of the Man is always a positive in my book, figuratively and literally speaking, or writing, or whatever. If you have ever heard the term, "blue sky" laws, you do not have to worry about it with a Rule 506 offering. That's not for nothing.

One last cool thing about Rule 506 is that you have options. There are two types of 506 offerings for private placement: 506(b) and 506(c). As you guessed, each has different criteria to meet in order to be exempted. Let's continue this incredibly exciting journey and jump into them!

Rule 506(b)

In times of uncertainty at sea, a wise captain will look for a port or harbor to dock his ship and wait out the weather or be safe from the enemy. Rule 506(b) is considered a "safe harbor" under Section 4(a)(2). I envision this little tidbit to be like protecting your security schooner from the Dread

Pirate Registration. You want to be protected because your little trading ship can carry more loot than many other ships because there is no limit to the amount of money you can raise under 506(b).

To outmaneuver the pirates and stay in the Section 4(a)(2) harbor, with its fine Rums and wonderful accordion-laden street music, your ship must fit specific requirements. First, you can't use general solicitation or advertising to market the security. Second, you may sell your security to an unlimited number of accredited investors, but you can only have thirty-five "sophisticated" investors. Third, you can be a bit stealthy in providing information to accredited investors, but you better be ready to give over financials to the sophisticated crowd. They must also receive everything that you communicated with the accrediteds as well. Finally, you must be available to answer questions by prospective purchasers.

I would like to help clear up some of the paragraph above. You are not permitted to use general solicitation. *What is it?* Great question. It is not defined, of course. Nothing is better than a term in a Rule that is left open for you to interpret while also permitting the SEC to interpret it. Guess whose interpretation wins? As best as I can tell (and again, I went to law school at night, so take this with a grain of salt), if you put the offering out on blast via social media or other mediums, you are violating the exemption. If you get sly and offer a seminar to learn about real estate and pump your upcoming property, you likely violated the exemption. Ask your smarter attorney, but I have a feeling that they will say the same thing.

To offer your security to a potential investor, you need to have a pre-existing relationship with them. A pre-existing relationship should have arisen from past business dealings, a social connection, or just getting to know the investor prior to saying, "Hey, you got $50k? I got a deal." There has to be some sincerity and time invested in knowing each other. Is your offering and bromance with your investor good enough to qualify? The SEC takes it on a case-by-case basis, but it appears that my suggestion can't hurt.[**]

You dodged the general solicitation landmine (it is a *great* feeling to dodge a solicitation charge, general or not) and your Rolodex is chock-full of pre-existing relationships. Who can get on your deal of a lifetime and take advantage of the 506(b) offering without destroying its exemption status? Accredited investors, that's who. *So...what is an accredited investor?* You can find the answer in 17 CFR

[**] Wilson Bradshaw LLP. "What Is a General Solicitation?" Wilson Bradshaw LLP, December 31, 2018. https://www.securitieslegal.com/general-solicitation-what-is-it/.

§230.501(a). In summary, an accredited investor is legally authorized to purchase securities that are not registered with regulatory authorities. They can buy private placement offerings.

Now, you are probably saying *You must have to be really smart to pass that test that they make you take to become accredited* (unless you already know this, then you are just saying, *No shit*)., Well, my friend, I have great news for you. There is no test. There are, however, some high financial standards to meet for a natural person. (1) You must have made $200k for the past two years with the expectation that the current year will be more of the same, or (2) You and your spouse combined for $300k in the same time frame, or (3) Your assets total over $1 million (excluding primary residence.) You don't test, you just are. Buddha would be smiling under his tree meditating on this. Note: *There are other types of accredited investors that are not natural persons.*

Hold on a second, it also states up to 35 "sophisticated" investors. Well, I used the popular term there; 17 CFR §230.506(b)(ii) actually states that "Each purchaser who is not an accredited investor either alone or with his purchaser representative(s) has such knowledge and experience in financial and business matters that he is capable of evaluating the merits and risks of the prospective investment, or the issuer reasonably believes immediately prior to making any sale that such purchaser comes within this description." So, technically, if you *really, really, really* wish it to be true, that friend who is on Twitter all the time and seems really smart can get in on your deal. Just kidding, I don't think that is the nature of the section.

You now have your rich homies and not-so-rich but educated homies on board with the idea of owning a sweet property. It is a 450-door community in the heart of the metroplex. You are a king. However, did you ever notice how many kings went crazy due to the threat of betrayal? Will your friends turn on you? Is that pre-existing relationship strong enough to keep them from telling your enemies your secrets? I bet you wish you would have fought harder to pick up the tab at dinner now. Luckily, 506(b) allows an issuer discretion on what information to provide if you keep false or misleading statements out of your communication. On the flip side, if you exclude information and that exclusion causes a false or misleading communication, you are a bad human and you violate 506(b).

Things are slightly different when you communicate with your smart but not rich investors. You must give them disclosure documents found in registered offerings like an offering circular or financial statements potentially audited by an accountant. Additionally, you can't keep any secrets from them that you did not keep from the accredited investor group. Really, if you value lasting relationships, this is not a big deal. The Private Placement Memorandum generally will contain all pertinent and important information regarding the nature of the business, nature of the property, potential risk, expected returns, and other important info for investors to consider.

One final note on 506(b). To remain docked in the fantastic harbor of safety, you need to present the owner of the dock a completed Form D within fifteen days of selling your first security. That will require you to give the owner information about your business, the people on your team, the types of securities that you offer, how much you are raising, and whatever other important information the form requires. Check it out for yourself.

Rule 506(c)

Sibling rivalry is a real thing. Maybe your sister was always prettier than you, or smarter. Maybe your brother was able to get better grades and make your parents love him more. I know that my brothers always tried to beat me in things, much in the same way the Washington Generals try to beat the Harlem Globetrotters. That's the rivalry between 506(b) and 506(c); 506(c) looks at 506(b) and thinks: *They think they are so cool. They raise all of this money and allow just anybody, up to thirty-five members of the poor group, to be a part of this? (B) even allows investors to self-certify. It uses the honor system for Christ's sake! 506(c) is bitter and exclusive.*

What kind of parties does 506(c) host in all its bitterness? The parties are open all year. There is no limit on money that can be raised in any twelve-month period. Sounds just like 506(b), but here is where 506(c) gets super petty. A (c) offering allows the party to be advertised publicly, like, "I'm having a bash. Bring your best glow sticks." However, there is a bouncer at the party that is checking IDs. If you are not accredited, you cannot go in, and fake IDs won't work...unless they are *really* good. The bouncer is going to take reasonable steps to ensure that anyone who says that they are accredited is in fact that.

So how many people can go to this super swank shindig? As many accredited investors as they want to have. There must be a Form D (17 CFR 239.500) filing fifteen days after the first party ticket is sold. The only issue for the party goer is that they can't leave the party (sell their interest) for a year (except for Exemption 4a7, which allows you to trade with another accredited investor). It has a Hotel California vibe. If they follow all of that, they don't have to worry about the mall cop/state security guys. No blue sky laws apply here. Federal law rules this fiesta. Finally, it would be wise for a 506(c) party to be covered by a Private Placement Memorandum in case the SEC decides to knock.

506(c) *does* have to worry about who enters the party though. Bad actor disqualifications will get that party shut down like parents returning early from vacation.

For now, that completes what I want to cover on Reg D. In the immortal words of Mr. Forest Gump, "That's all I got to say about that."

REG A PLUS

Yes, I know. "A" comes before "D" in the alphabet. Stop being a jerk. I placed Reg D first because it is the most popular exempt offering. It is pretty easy to set up, offer, and the state can't mess with you. Why would anyone care about another type of security offering? Well, you still must file that Form D and B. The securities are restricted and can't be sold on the open market without the company registering, which defeats the purpose of a Reg D offering.

There is very much a "Don't try this at home" feel to Reg A. It is not for beginners. It was created by the JOBS Act as part of Title IV to allow qualifying companies to offer securities through equity crowdfunding. You guessed it;

a complicated definition creates a paper heavy offering. Due to the paperwork and reporting burden, Reg A offerings are generally limited to companies prepared to foot that bill. We are talking mid-stage companies and startups with a great consumer base. More succinct, Reg A only makes sense if you are raising over $4 million when balancing cost and time. The good news is that once your offering is complete, your investors can resell their securities without delay. They are not stuck waiting like a Reg D participant.

One last thing. There are seven states that will **not** allow you to raise funds through a Reg A offering without a broker-dealer (B-D) being involved. A B-D is a natural person, company, or other organization that engages in the business of trading securities for its own account or on the behalf of its customers. (Lemke and Lins, *Soft Dollars and Other Trading Activities* (Thomson West, 2013-2014 ed.). If you use a FINRA-approved B-D, you can raise capital wherever your heart desires. If you do not, you will need to be very careful in offering your investment to residents of Texas, Florida, New Jersey, Nevada, Arizona, and North Dakota. You could possibly work with a securities attorney from those states early in the process. It will potentially delay your offering, but you "could" avoid the fees charged by a B-D. If you are from Florida, that may not be an option.

Reg A comes in two tiers, creatively titled Tier 1 and Tier 2. Like all things in life, there are positives and negatives that come along with your choice. Choose wisely.

TIER 1

The first thing to know about a Tier 1 offering is that you are required to mess with state blue sky laws. That requires you to obtain state-by-state exemptions to those blue beauties. If there is one thing that we can all agree on, state governments are extremely inefficient. If the idea of dealing with understaffed and antiquated government does not turn you off, then let's dig deeper.

On top of dealing with state-level requirements, a Tier 1 issuer has quite a few document obligations to the Big Boss. You will need to file a for 1-A as well as provide two years of financial statements. You are not required to complete an audit before filing, however, nor do you need to provide an annual audit to the SEC. You *do* have to create an offering circular, but you have three format choices. Additionally, you do not have to provide Exchange Act reports until you have 500 shareholders and $10 million in assets. That is to the SEC though; your state, or any state that you accept investors from, may require all of those. That is why this tier is predominately used by banks.

What do I get for all this extra work? A $20 million cap on raises each twelve-month period. *Wait, what?* I just read about the Reg Ds, and those caps were unlimited. Why would I deal with such a major headache and be limited in what I can raise? I'm not a sadist...most of the time and depending on the partner.

It does not seem to make sense until you think about market supply. How many accredited investors are there in the U.S.? According to the website, Don't Quit Your Day Job, microdata from the Federal Reserve shows that there were 13,665,475 in 2019.*** One in ten households qualify as accredited. Sweet, but what about the other 365ish million in the country? That's who Reg A Tier 1 allows you to reach.

Okay, now I'm torn. I would like to cast a wider net, but I do not want to deal with state oversight. What to do, what to do? There is a website in the footnotes that will allow you to make an educated decision based on state filing requirements.****

*** "Finance and Investing Tools, Calculators, Research, and More," DQYDJ, September 5, 2020, http://www.dqydj.com/.

**** "State Filing Requirements: Regulation A," NASAA, https://www.nasaa.org/industry-resources/securities-issuers/coordinated-review/regulation-a-offerings/state-filing-requirements/.

TIER 2

You know how they tell a guy who is down on his luck attracting a soul mate that there is "someone out there for everyone?" That is Tier 1. It takes a special match to accept the annoying traits of meeting all those state level blue sky requirements. Tier 2 is more attractive to investors, much in the same way that Brad Pitt is more attractive than this author. In general, Brad Pitt has a more symmetrical face, prominent chin and cheekbones, fuller lips, and a nose that isn't bent in the middle. His teeth are probably smaller than mine and don't require an hour to brush properly. Most people would pick him to go out with. I can't blame them. I also can't blame them for picking Tier 2 of Reg A.

For starters, you can raise way more money under Tier 2, as in $55 million more. You can, for the most part, avoid the most annoying trait of Tier 1, dealing with the in-laws...er, "blue sky" laws for each state that one of your investors live in. For my fellow law folks, the offering is preempted from state securities registration. Even better? If you keep your number of investors to under 300, you can stop ongoing reporting to the SEC by filing a Form 1-Z exit report!

Fewer hoops to jump through is a major benefit, but it is not the only benefit. For my crypto folks out in the crowd your investors can invest with cryptocurrencies if you permit it.

Imagine being a 25-year-old who bought eight Bitcoin for $85 in 2012 and never stopped adding here and there. That kid is now a 34-year-old multimillionaire. They need tax havens, and they need to diversify. With the explosion of new millionaires holding most of their net worth in crypto, this is a real investor class. Tier 2 is perfect for them.

Finally, you can promote your offering like all the big boys and girls out there. You are permitted to generally solicit money. If you have a kick-ass marketing campaign, you can push your property until the round fills. Wait, there's more. You do not need to rely only on accredited investors. Sure, accredited investors are not limited in what they can purchase, but that isn't the best part. If you hurry now, you can also lock down non-accredited investors at a low introductory offer. Disclaimer, they can't invest more than 10 percent of their annual income or net worth. Disclaimer to the disclaimer, they *can* if the securities will be listed on a national securities exchange after qualifying. Keep that in mind.

Alas, like the beautiful prom queen you somehow convinced to be your significant other, beautiful things can get...less beautiful. There are drawbacks. Just like your pretty little queen, Tier 2 offerings can be complicated. You will have to deal with the drama of dealing with high maintenance...record keeping. If you are an attentive person anyway, high maintenance is not an issue. If you are just trying to live your best life, it can be a hassle. You will need to file annual, semi-annual, and current reports with the SEC.

On top of that, they will go through your phone *a lot*. Be ready for the strict audit requirements. Just as they may even tell you to edit your social media posts, the financial statements in your offering circular must be audited. Be prepared to say, "No, you look beautiful," a lot.

I, one day, hope to raise my daughter to be a beautiful person, inside and out. She may or may not be a prom queen, but she will be high-ish maintenance because she will demand respect. A young man, or woman, will need my permission as well. I'm going on that first date to the movies as the driver unless I know you are a great driver and know that 11 p.m. means 11 p.m. What does this have to do with this? If you haven't understood the meshing of storylines here, you need a chaperone. To qualify as an exempt offering, Tier 2 requires you to hire a transfer agent registered with the SEC.

Even though the paperwork is a pain and the offering is a bit labor-intensive, the benefits are immense. No restrictions on the resale of securities and access for non-accredited investors provide a lower risk, more inclusive offering. It opens a bigger market of potential investors. It's beautiful.

REGULATION CROWDFUNDING

Much like kids of the social media age live on abbreviations, so too did the SEC with Regulation Crowdfunding. If you were to tweet about it, you'd type "Reg CF." I have teenagers; this is accurate, I know. Reg CF itself, in my eyes, is like the hipster. It's new; it's trendy. It has a beard faded perfectly into a haircut. It wears tight jeans that it rolls at the bottom regardless of body type. It wears plaid shirts everywhere. It may even wear glasses even though a prescription is not necessary. It, for sure, has arms full of meaningless tattoos. What is the good and bad of this trendy new offering? Let's pretend that we are sitting at our local brewery sipping on an IPA, because that's all that's available, and discuss.

Becoming a hipster is not easy if you like options. You really must give into conformity and not break with the group. Ideas are pretty much okay if the group agrees with them. That's kind of like a Reg CF offering. To be exempt, your transactions must be online through an SEC-registered intermediary, either a broker-dealer or a funding portal. You must also file Form C, two years of certified and audited financials, and annual progress reports. If you step out of line, you lose exemption, much as you lose your ability to be a condescending patron at the local brewery.

There are positives to being a hipster. You get to live in a world where you are an altruistic king. You can raise $5 million in twelve months and open that up to non-accredited investors. You just do not believe that they can think completely on their own and must be protected. Therefore, you limit the amount that they can invest. Your hipster-approved clique of accrediteds can invest as much as they want. Once they have purchased the offering, neither group can resell their securities for twelve months.

I was perhaps harsh on hipsters. They are just people trying to find their way in this big, tough world. If wearing jeans a size too small and spending way too much time looking just right at getting that "I don't care what I look like" look is their thing, then so be it. I believe, however, that they should be given time to ask around and see if the look suits them. Reg CF gives them that chance. Before filing Form C, you can "test the waters" to gauge interest in your potential offering. Just like when you purchase the jeans, you can still ask people how you look in them on a limited basis, like taking a picture and not making the post public, you can solicit investors with limits on the advertising.

It will be interesting to see how Reg CF develops as the number of funding portals increases. I suspect that, much in the same way that the hipster gets tired of being a barista and strives for more, the offering limits will increase. With its limited oversight, Reg CF could become a Tier 2 light for particularly real estate investors who are used to tying their money up for over twelve months. A $5 million raise potentially buys a $25 million property. Skinny jeans or not, that should be solid cash flow.

Wrapping it UP with a Nice Table

Types of Fundraising Exemptions				
	How much can I raise?	Disclosure Required	Who can invest?	Can I advertise?
Regulation Crowdfunding*	$5,000,000	Medium	Anyone	Yes
Regulation D, Rule 506b	unlimited	Low	The Rich**	No***
Regulation D, Rule 506c	unlimited	Low	The Rich**	Yes
Regulation A+	$75 million	High	Anyone	Yes

*If you end up raising more than $5M in your Reg CF raise, we'll spin up a concurrent Regulation D, Rule 506(c) offering so you can raise an unlimited amount from accredited investors. We support 506c raises only when the issuer is also doing a Reg CF offering.

**Rich means *accredited investors* with $1M+ in net worth (minus their home) or who've earned more than $200K per year ($300k with spouse) in each of the past 2 years. It also means institutions like banks and VCs. Investors must verify their accredited status to invest under Reg D.[*****]

***** "Legal Primer for Founders," Wefunder, https://help.wefunder.com/legal-primer.